THINKING

THE

UNTHINKABLE

W9-BPN-486

146

THINKING
THE
UNTHINKABLE

JOHN
WESLEY WHITE

CREATION
HOUSE

Creation House
Strang Communications Company
600 Rinehart Road
Lake Mary, FL 32746
(407) 333-0600

First printing, February 1992
Second printing, September 1992
Third printing, October 1992

CONTENTS

Foreword 7

Preface 9

1 "Wars and Rumours of Wars" 15

2 "All Sorts of Armour" 24

3 The Nuclear Threat 31

4 Doom in Every Corner 41

5 "From One End of Heaven to the Other" 52

6 The Witness of Science 60

7 "Never Able to Grasp the Truth" 71

8 A Whole Lot of Shaking Going On 83

9 "There Shall Be Famines" 91

10 Feasting During Famine 100

11 "Antichrist Shall Come" 108

12 "Israel Shall Be Saved" 119

13 Countdown in Israel 130

14 "Gog, the Land of Magog" 139

15 "Abomination of Desolation" 152

16 The Reign of the Beast 162

17 Appointment With Armageddon 171

18 The Reign of King Jesus 182

19 Everlasting Fire 193

20 "I Will Come Again" 202

FOREWORD

SCRIPTURE EXHORTS us to pray for peace, to seek peace, to pursue peace and at all times to hope for peace. Jesus pronounced a special blessing on peacemakers. Routine wishes for a world at peace come from Buckingham Palace, from the Heavenly Gate in Beijing, from the Kremlin and from the White House. Pope John Paul says that all men and women of good will are to aspire for peace. "We must want it at any cost," he says.

But is it realistic to expect peace? Whether you read the literature of diagnosis or prognosis, it seems that, as pundit Jack McArthur observes, you encounter "almost solid gloom and disaster." Good men throughout the ages have tried admirably to avoid an impending Armageddon, but to little avail. Rabbi Reuben Slonim notes that religion historically has "promised to abolish war, establish the equality of all men, prohibit the exploitation of human beings and transform the City of Man into the City of God. Despite the collective efforts of all cults and creeds, the sword is still the sword, not a ploughshare." With $1 trillion a year earmarked for global weaponry and death machines, the rabbi's point is well made.

This march toward destruction is not without hope.

Jesus Christ promises, "Let not your heart be troubled...[for] I will come again, and receive you unto myself" (John 14:1,3). God the Son will return to earth from heaven to fulfill the prayer His disciples have uttered through the ages: "Thy kingdom come. Thy will be done in earth, as it is in heaven" (Matt. 6:10).

Anticipating Christ's return is the business of all believers. The apostle Paul defined a Christian as one who has "turned to God from idols to serve the living and true God; and to wait for his Son from heaven" (1 Thess. 1:9b-10a). A study of current events, as John Wesley White shows in this book, demonstrates that we could very well be living close to what the Bible repeatedly calls the "time of the end."

To those who are Christians, I hope this book will arouse obedience to the prophecy of Joel, to "put ye in the sickle, for the harvest is ripe: come, get you down; for the press is full.... Multitudes, multitudes [are] in the valley of decision" (Joel 3:13-14). Let us go everywhere, as Jesus exhorted, and preach the gospel to all nations, and "then shall the end come" (Matt. 24:14).

If you are not a Christian, my prayer is that *Thinking the Unthinkable* will cause you to respond positively to Jesus' question "What think ye of Christ?" (Matt. 22:42) and consequently to pray according to His promise: "Whosoever shall call upon the name of the Lord shall be saved" (Rom. 10:13).

Billy Graham
Montreat, North Carolina

A POPULAR song a few years ago envisaged "there's a new world comin.' " Is there? As 1992 is ushered in, the Americas are celebrating the five hundredth anniversary of the discovery of our "new world."

This is also the year the Old World of Western Europe achieved the biblically predicted consummation of its apolitical as well as economic reunion. The Treaty of Rome in thirty-five years has evolved via the European Common Market into a literal revived Roman Empire. But in stark contrast what for seventy-four years has been the USSR is no more. Sitting here in Russia as I am during the first week of 1992, U.S. Secretary of State James Baker on "Face the Nation" has warned the world solemnly that what we had known as the USSR could well be on the verge of a civil war along the lines of what is happening in Yugoslavia, the difference being that the contesting republics could well resort to using some of their stockpile of twenty-seven thousand nuclear weapons. Mikhail Gorbachev agrees, lamenting that such a struggle would make the Yugoslavian bloodbath like a joke in comparison.

So is there a new world comin'? Yes, thank God, it

is — in the second coming of Jesus Christ.

I am writing this preface with a trembling hand and an aching heart. Just a few weeks ago Kathleen and I said good-bye, insofar as life here on earth is concerned, to John Wesley White Jr., a pilot whose plane crashed, resulting in his instant ascent forever to be with the Lord. Earlier in his life, traveling with his mother, brothers and me from Scotland to California, he had played his trumpet and sung:

> When the trumpet of the Lord shall sound, and
>   time shall be no more,
> And the morning breaks, eternal, bright and
>   fair;
> When the saved of earth shall gather over on
>   the other shore,
> And the roll is called up yonder, I'll be there.

So Wesley is home!

And so shall all believers on the Lord Jesus Christ be one glad day, perhaps sooner than we think. In fact, Jesus assured us that in an hour that we think not, the Son of Man will come. In His final benediction to John the aged, He announced, "Behold, I come quickly" (Rev. 22:12). John's reply was the same as Kathleen's and mine is at this sad moment: "Amen! Even so, come, Lord Jesus" (v. 20).

Such a blessed hope is not the mere fancy of a fertile imagination. It is the assurance of Scripture. Jesus promised His inquiring disciples that man would edge toward annihilation, but before he slipped over the precipice Christ would return to evacuate His children home, forever to be with the Lord.

Time, having earlier run a cover story titled "Thinking the Unthinkable," noted in its October 7, 1991, issue that it's "almost unthinkable" that man is at "the nuclear brink [in] a world bristling with nuclear weapons ready for instant launch." President George Bush had just made his speech pledging that the United States would lead the way, it is hoped, to eliminating those "little" tactical nuclear weapons while protecting key elements of the U.S. war machine: the B-2 Stealth bomber, the Trident II submarine and the Star Wars antimissile defense.

According to the *Time* article, the president was really saying to the Soviet Union, "Let's get rid of the mainstays of your nuclear arsenal, but not of ours." Bush was responding to concern in the West about the collapse of the Soviet Union and the possibility that dissident groups may mishandle nuclear weapons.

A case in point was when a band of rebels broke into an installation in Azerbaijan at which nuclear devices were stored. Noted one of the U.S. administration officials: "We've got the makings of (veritable) hell...a Tom Clancy novel."

Time lamented that the Soviet arsenal was spread around several republics which are now emerging as countries with their own agendas, not at all above bartering bombs for butter. Of the fifteen republics, five minor ones are abandoning the "Union." Of the ten that remain, six have a Muslim majority, the Islamic fundamentalists casting their allegiance with their Muslim brotherhood in and around the Middle East. *Time* is candid. There are "plenty of people in Moscow — not all of them in uniform — who are desperate to cling to Soviet strategic nuclear strength." *Time* also noted that Britain and France have independent nuclear forces and have shown little interest in reducing their stockpiles while China, India, Israel and persistent Iraq are going all out to upgrade and expand theirs.

Sums up the October 7 *Time*: There's no disguising the worldwide "nightmare of cataclysmic thinkers [fearing] nuclear annihilation resulting from some accidental slip — a wayward blip on a radar screen perhaps — that would precipitate the launch of weapons kept on hair-trigger alert."

One month earlier, drawing a bead on the failed Soviet coup, *Time* (September 9, 1991) concluded the future suddenly looks problematic and dangerous. "What of the 27,000 nuclear warheads deployed on missiles, bombers, submarines and at ammunition dumps across the old Union?"

Fears of the unknown bring out predictions of apocalypse. "Dick Elkus, an advisory board member of the Washington-based Center for Strategic and International Studies, predicted, 'What has happened so far is a 6.0 earthquake on its way to becoming an 8.3 — 900 times greater,' " *Time* reported. "The Harriman Institute's Richard Ericson said, 'We are facing what is perhaps the largest man-made disaster the world has ever seen.' "

Our time, in the long history of the world, is the most dangerous time ever for the human race. Vincent Cannistraro, a former CIA chief, announced in 1991 that scientists are on the verge of developing a virus that could destroy humanity. Harvard professor Bernard Lown laments that mankind is doomed, locked into a "race to Armageddon."

Such somber sentiments surface even in the glittering world of celebrity, as actress Barbra Streisand commented in *Esquire* magazine: "I do believe that the world is coming to an end. I just feel that science, technology, and the mind have surpassed the soul — the heart. There is no balance in terms of feeling and love for fellow man."

Only months earlier, at the dawn of the 1990s, such comments would have been out of place. Experts — whether statesmen, scientists, social reformers or even theologians — were writing that the prospects for a new world order had not been as bright since the post-Napoleonic era, early in the nineteenth century. With the collapse of communism it seemed that the idea of peace was the dominant mood of universal man.

Not much time elapsed before the rose-tinted glasses were taken off. Saddam Hussein broke the bubble of apparent peace on August 2, 1990, when he invaded Kuwait. Desert Shield and the subsequent Operation Desert Storm prompted *Time* to run a longer-than-ever sequence of back-to-back cover stories on war. Before his death, which occurred in the wake of Hussein's charge into Kuwait, B.F. Skinner, renowned behaviorist and dean of Harvard University's Department of Psychology, demanded angrily: "Why are we not acting to save the world?" Remonstrating before a convention of the American Psychological Society, he said, "Is there to be much more history at all?" The world is "fatally ill.... The argument that we have always solved our problems in the past and shall, therefore, solve this one is like reassuring a dying man by pointing out that he has always recovered from his illness."

The purpose of this book is to answer the question, Is man's destiny life or death? Is each individual free to choose life, or is he or she doomed to be liquidated in a nuclear holocaust? That is why we have here assembled numerous perspectives from strategically positioned world leaders in politics, economics, science, philosophy and theology. Many of their comments, willingly or unwillingly, pertain to Scripture regarding Christ's return and the end of this age. The Bible is clear that history has moved continually toward a definite climax. Are we in fact closer than many realize to the return of Jesus Christ and the end of the present world order as we know it?

John Wesley White, D. Phil. (Oxford University)
Toronto, Canada

ONE

"WARS AND RUMOURS OF WARS"

SOON JESUS would be gone. Peter, Andrew, James and John did not fully understand this, but just prior to His trial and crucifixion they asked Him what would be the scenario leading to His return and the end of the age. Jesus replied that there would be wars and rumors of wars with nation rising up against nation and kingdom against kingdom. Conditions would rapidly deteriorate into such widespread holocaust that the extermination of the whole human race would occur unless Christ returned.

John had a generation to reflect on Jesus' words. Then, providing greater insight into the last days, he received the revelation that makes up the last book of the Bible. He foretells of the coming Antichrist who, after a brief period of peace, will declare war (Rev. 11:7). This war will lead to his world conquest so that for a short time he will "rule over all nations and language groups" (Rev. 13:7, TLB). But a massive revolt occurs as miracle-working demons conspire with the world rulers to gather their armies for a great battle near a Middle Eastern site called Armageddon (Rev. 16:13-16).

Biblical prophecy and current events lead us to ask two critical questions. *Are the existing armaments capable of inflicting a terminal war that could fulfill the Bible's prophecy of Armageddon?* It needs to be pointed out that currently there is a large enough stockpile of weapons as to precipitate just such an apocalypse. *Has the world rounded the last bend and entered the final lap leading toward Armageddon?* Many perceive that it has. We will see, as we explore world developments coinciding with prophetic Scripture, that there is strong reason to expect harbingers of Armageddon to emerge on the horizon at any time.

In the end Jesus Christ will save His remnant who know Him. But if you do not know Jesus Christ as your personal Savior, no amount of insight into these end-times developments will make a difference in your eternal destiny. If you have committed your life to Christ, may the awareness of this exciting fulfillment of prophecy impel you to share the gospel with those who are perishing spiritually.

The Great Tribulation

Throughout history Armageddon has been the term used to describe a final war of mankind between the forces of good and evil, those of God versus those of the devil. Its expectation is common to Judaism, Christianity, Islam and most other major religions. There are variations in the scenario, but in each version God prevails.

My interpretation of Scripture is that Armageddon is the finale of a "great tribulation" of seven years. During this period the world's political, social, economic and moral conditions will worsen.

As a result of the rapture of the church (1 Thess. 4:13-16), a half-billion believers will be gone, many of them from North America. The geopolitical balance will shift dramatically. Almost immediately after the rapture of the church the Russian military, joined by Euro-Asian satellites and instigating Islamic nations (named in Ezekiel 38), will descend on Israel. Their goal will be to exterminate the Jewish people or drive them out of their land. A regional nuclear war will ensue, in which 85 percent of the attacking coalition forces — led by the Russians — will perish. Then the Antichrist, also known as the beast, will emerge in Europe as a great leader. His first step will be to sign a peace pact with Israel.

A three-and-a-half-year period of comparative peace will follow, after which a three-and-a-half-year period of cataclysmic war will take place. The Antichrist will be the focus of worldwide attention during this conflict. During this the "unthinkable" will take place: two-thirds of the human race will be killed, followed by Armageddon, in which all the armies of the world will clash, resolved to settle forever who is to rule the earth.

The Present Unfolding

Can we measure where we are in terms of God's plan for history? The answer is no and yes. No, because the Bible tells us to expect surprises. Paul wrote, "That day of the Lord will come unexpectedly like a thief in the night. When people are saying, 'All is well, everything is quiet and peaceful' — then, all of a sudden, disaster will fall upon them as suddenly as a woman's birth pains begin when her child is born. And these people will not be able to get away anywhere — there will be no place to hide" (1 Thess. 5:2-3, TLB).

In retrospect, though, we may have recently lived through just such a period where widespread peace was followed by a sudden shaking.

Hillel Schwartz, in a scholarly article in the August 6, 1990, issue of *The New Republic*, wrote that the biblical literalists who trumpeted a "pre-millennial, pre-tribulation rapture" had become passé by 1990. He predicted that history would show that biblical literalists peaked in 1983 but by 1989 to 1990 the idea of biblical apocalypse had been swept aside. With "the quiet exit of the cold war, we may no longer have constant nightmares of global nuclear exchange."

Of course, four days prior to August 6 (when the article by Schwartz was already in print) the nightmares returned. Iraq invaded Kuwait, and the entire world focused on the Middle East. *The Los Angeles Times* foresaw "an all-out war" in the Middle East, while *The Toronto Sun* on September 4 expressed fear of "a general war in which nuclear weapons might be used by both sides."

After the Gulf War Mohammad Saad Al Sailai, Kuwait's United Nations representative, observed, "We will never be as trusting as we were, because we were living in a dream world." Was it truly a dream world? Or can mankind pick up from where it left off on August 1, 1990?

As remarkable and quick as the victory was in Kuwait and Iraq, it by no means tidied up all the problems in that region. The Shiite Muslims in southern Iraq were resolved to turn their country into an Islamic republic like Iran. Millions of Kurds were trying desperately to insurrect a revolt but were crushed ruthlessly. Tens of thousands died at the hands of Saddam's army immediately after defeat in Kuwait. Millions of Kurdish refugees were pushing their way out of the mountains into Turkey and Iran, embittered that the United Nations coalition did not eliminate Saddam Hussein.

Armageddon Awareness

Now that it's behind us, we know that the Gulf War was not Armageddon. During the Desert Shield stage people were less certain. A Gallup poll found 15 percent of Americans thought that Armageddon was brewing; surely many more gave some careful thought to the matter.

There is no doubt but that apocalyptic war has been increasingly on people's minds. For years I have appeared on radio and television shows around the world, but not until February 11, 1991, did I find myself part of an "Examination of Armageddon Theology" program on the very secular Canadian Broadcasting Corporation. The following month the Associated Press distributed to its thousands of member newspapers a lengthy article on Armageddon. On *USA TODAY's* September 21, 1990, editorial page, Barbara Reynolds noted the proliferation of "eschatological language: the Antichrist, 666, the millennium, the rapture. Biblical prophets from Daniel to John [foresaw] apocalypse, probably a nuclear or biological holocaust." Christian magazines, too, all clocked in with their pieces on the Middle East conflict and how it pertained to prophecy.

The possible approach of the final curtain on this present age is not confined to the masses who read these periodicals. World statesmen are also concerned. In fact, it seems they have never been so discouraged with regard to the prospects for world peace.

Mankind seems to "drift towards World War III," agonized United Nations Secretary General Javier Perez de Cuellar on CNN News, January 15, 1991. "After fifty years of diplomacy, at seventy years of age, I am discouraged."

"We prepare for war like precocious giants, and for peace like retarded pygmies," said Douglas Roche, Canadian ambassador for disarmament, quoting Nobel Peace Prize winner Lester B. Pearson.

Edward Shevardnadze, Soviet foreign minister from

1985-1990, noted in 1991 how two years earlier the Soviets had been on "the brink of a third world war," ready to unleash all of their weaponry to keep their empire intact.

The Russian Connection

Shevardnadze's admission is no small piece in this puzzle. A close reading of Scripture, as later chapters will detail, shows that *it will be Russia into whose jaws the fanatical fundamentalist Muslims will put hooks and draw into a war on Israel*. One might argue that the Israelis could strike a peace accord, negotiated by the Soviets and the Americans under the umbrella of the United Nations. But the Bible teaches that this will not happen until the emergence of the Antichrist. Therefore we must not let current events dupe us into believing the Soviet Union is on a clear path toward peace.

Mikhail Gorbachev survived the 1991 coup that attempted to re-establish a hard-line, conservative communist government. Yet Gorbachev remains a paradox. As the late Andrei Gromyko assessed him, will the world see his "nice smile" or his "iron teeth"? With half of the Soviet Union's gross national product spent on the military — a vertically integrated, that is, self-contained complex — the nation remains well-situated to play a major role in the impending apocalypse.

The Gulf War put the Soviet Union in a delicate position because Iraq has been its client state for a quarter of a century. The *Rocky Mountain News* (Denver, Colorado) observed on April 8, 1991, "President Mikhail Gorbachev showed a strange eagerness to preserve Iraq's military might when he pushed for an early halt to the war and later balked at requiring the destruction of Baghdad's ballistic missiles." A later chapter will explore how Russia and Iraq will be allied with Libya in the events leading to Armageddon.

The Nuclear Itch

Throughout the second half of the 1980s there was minimal discussion of the existence and potential of atomic, hydrogen, neutron, bacteriological, biological, chemical and other bombs. No one wanted to rock the boat. After all, Gorbachev was ending the cold war almost single-handedly.

People who give any thought to world affairs will now have to take off their rose-tinted glasses. Though the Gulf War was limited to conventional warfare, everyone worried about Iraq's biological and chemical arsenal. After the war Iraq's nuclear capacity came under close international scrutiny.

William Beecher, Washington bureau chief for *The Minneapolis Star Tribune*, having studied worldwide disarmament progress, concluded in 1990 that "nuclear arsenals are essentially undiminished." Ten new hydrogen bombs are manufactured somewhere in the world every day.

The United States was the first to use nuclear weapons but has exercised considerable restraint regarding any further use, all the while building up its arsenal. This sentiment, though, appears to be changing. During Desert Storm 45 percent of Americans said they would favor using nuclear weapons if they might save the lives of U.S. troops, and there was consideration of the same at the highest levels of government. Perhaps such a move in some cases would have spared many lives, but one thing is sure — the precedent it set would have been a step along the road to Armageddon.

Of more concern than potential U.S. use of nuclear

bombs is what many other countries might do. As many as forty-four nations are in the process of assembling the component parts of a nuclear bomb. Iraq was in that process during Desert Storm, and most observers believe Saddam Hussein would have detonated a nuclear bomb over Israel if he had had one finished. His efforts to develop his nuclear capacity remain obsessive, undiminished and at this point unsubordinated.

Man's Dark Side

"From whence come wars?" asked the apostle James. "Come they not hence, even of your lusts that war in your members? Ye lust, and have not: ye kill, and desire to have, and cannot obtain: ye fight and war, yet ye have not" (James 4:1-2). The psalmist, speaking of the warmonger, wrote, "The words of his mouth were smoother than butter, but war was in his heart" (Ps. 55:21).

What pertinent commentary for moderns! The ancient wisdom imparted by the Holy Spirit in Scripture revealed man's propensity for war. It continues to be an integral part of today's thinkers. In his 1990 book *The Undiscovered Self*, the great psychoanalyst Carl G. Jung theorized that unless humankind is prepared to deal with the "shadow side" of his nature, there's no way war can be avoided. Albert Einstein, whose discoveries led to the invention of the nuclear bomb, was so worried about the repercussions of his work that he wrote to psychologist Sigmund Freud. Did he think man could resist the proclivity to war? No, Freud replied, he did not think so.

Spokesmen for diverse religious beliefs also expect Armageddon or the return of Christ, or both, to be imminent.

Participating with me on the "Examination of Armageddon Theology" panel was Sajikda Alvi, professor of

Islamic history at McGill University in Montreal. Basing her views on the Koran, Dr. Alvi agreed that Jesus would be returning and that prior to His coming there would be unprecedented evil, terrifying disturbances in nature and the appearance of the most demon-possessed man in all history. All this would culminate in the worst war ever, which she said could be called Armageddon.

Also on the panel was Canada's Tom Harpur, an Oxford-trained Anglican clergyman, liberal writer and outspoken Universalist. He lamented that just as it appeared we were "on our way to an end to war and a millennium of peace," it appears we're going "in exactly the opposite direction." He said, "The world is hurtling towards a conflagration worse than anything we have seen."

A rapidly growing Orthodox Jewish movement anticipates the Messiah will come soon. An article in *The Grand Forks Herald* (North Dakota) on September 9, 1990, during the Desert Shield buildup, said these Jews believe "what is going on in Iraq is definitely a sign of the imminent arrival of the Messiah." They expect the Messiah to arrive in Israel to bring "redemption [and] a period of complete peace and harmony."

But before this era of light dawns there is some darkness to experience. History cannot escape Armageddon.

TWO

"ALL SORTS OF ARMOUR"

IRAQ AND Kuwait in ancient times were known as Chaldea and Mesopotamia or — at the peak of their power — as Babylonia and Babylon. The Garden of Eden was there. Noah built the ark there. It was where the matrix of civilization was gestated, where the many languages and races of people had their origin.

Wheeled vehicles, multistoried buildings, metal tools and machinery, grains, fruits, vegetables, reading, writing, arithmetic, politics, economics, science and philosophy emanated from there. It was the astonishingly advanced culture from which Abraham came and where Daniel and Ezekiel wrote their prophecies. Babylon as a city, a nation and an empire is mentioned nearly three hundred times in the Scriptures from Genesis to Revelation.

So when Saddam Hussein reunited Iraq and Kuwait by brutal force for seven months after they had been separate countries for two generations, it was no surprise to students of Bible prophecy that they should become the focus of world attention. Babylon is conspicuous in what the Bible tells us will yet happen there, just as it has been in history.

As we will see, the brief events of Desert Storm bear remarkable kinship with prophecies such as Ezekiel 38:4's "all sorts of armour" and Revelation 18's prediction of a dramatic fall of Babylon. The question arises: Was Desert Storm a complete fulfillment of such Scripture? No. But just as World War I served as a precursor to World War II — because the "German problem" was unresolved by the armistice of post-1918 — so it should be no surprise if Saddam Hussein or his successor rises to stir even greater trouble in the Middle East.

We would be naive to dismiss the 1990-1991 developments in the Middle East as having no relationship to God's revelation of the end times. Desert Storm may be over, but the hurricane is yet to come.

Death and Mourning

John, in his book of Revelation, foresaw Babylon's role in the time of the end: "Babylon the great is fallen, is fallen, and is become the habitation of devils, and the hold of every foul spirit.... the merchants of the earth are waxed rich through the abundance of her [resources. On the other hand]...her sins have reached unto heaven, and God hath remembered her iniquities.... How much she hath glorified herself, and lived deliciously.... Therefore shall her plagues come in one day, death, and mourning, and famine; and she shall be utterly burned with fire.... The [rulers] of the earth...shall bewail her...when they shall see the smoke of her burning, standing afar off for the fear of her torment...for in one hour is thy judgment come. And the merchants of the earth shall weep and mourn over her; for no man buyeth their merchandise any more" (Rev. 18:2-11).

A few years ago such a prophecy seemed ponderous. No longer. Seeing the "smoke of her burning" was certainly true enough for modern-day Babylon as Desert Storm concluded. *USA TODAY*'s prediction on January 15, 1991, the eve of the Gulf War, was an overstatement, but it reflected scientists' concerns: "Smoke from the burning oil could block sunlight, lower temperatures by as much as 68 degrees Fahrenheit within 1,000 miles of Kuwait. [It] could disrupt monsoons throughout India, Asia and Africa, causing crop failures for up to 1 billion people." In reality the smoke from the hundreds of burning wells continued for months and brought with it serious environmental problems, though not as dramatic as *USA TODAY* predicted.

Desert Storm also provided a foretaste of the "death and mourning" prophesied in Revelation 18 that is to come in Babylon. There is no minimizing of the bloodletting that took place. *The New York Times* editorialized, "No man can see the picture or hear the accounts of this human suffering — men, women, and most painfully of all, innocent children — and not be deeply moved."

Iraq's estimated fatalities were one hundred thousand to two hundred thousand, possibly higher. Compared with coalition deaths, the casualty ratio was three thousand to one. If it hadn't been for the accidental deaths the coalition inflicted on its own soldiers, the ratio would have been as high as ten thousand to one.

The Gulf War was a long stride down the road to Armageddon. Astute observers around the world realized that if a devil-driven Saddam Hussein single-handedly instigated that much havoc, what might a biblically prophesied Antichrist do?

A Debut of Weapons

When the bombing of Baghdad began on January 17, there rained down "more explosives on Iraq in fourteen hours than fell on Hiroshima," according to *The Toronto Star*. There were 80,000 bombing sorties by the coalition forces, the 66,487 bombs being *twice as many as were dropped during the whole of World Wars I and II combined*, the *Star* reported. But what makes that figure even more mind-boggling is that Pentagon sources claim that because these were "smart bombs," as they've come to be known because of their pinpoint accuracy, "one ton of explosives unleashed in the Persian Gulf is as effective as 18,000 tons of World War II bombs," according to the *Star*. Not only were the instruments of destruction used in high numbers, but they included many of the newest and most sophisticated weaponry ever deployed — echoing the Ezekiel 38:4 reference to "all sorts of armour." The United States alone employed forty-two weapons systems never before tested in warfare.

Of all the guns ever developed, the multiple launch rocket system (MLR) is by far the most devastating. It fires twelve rockets simultaneously. Each rocket carries 644 bomblets, or submunitions. Any of these can tear into tanks, armored personnel carriers, trucks or human beings.

But what apparently did most of the killing in Desert Storm were the fuel-air-explosive bombs. FAE creates a fine mist of highly flammable fuel that ignites as soon as it envelops the target. The resulting blast is five times more powerful than TNT. It sucks all the oxygen from the air, thus asphyxiating troops sheltered in trenches or bunkers. This weapon is capable of exterminating all life in a radius of up to three miles. News reports have speculated that four out of five Iraqi military deaths could be attributed to these FAEs.

Molecular Menace

Of all the "sorts of armour" being developed, one of the most frightening is chemical warfare. These weapons of mass destruction are also known as biological or bacteriological bombs, often referred to as "the poor man's atomic bombs."

Anyone who doubts their reality need only ask the millions of Israelis who, during January and February 1991, had to jam themselves into bomb shelters and put on gas masks for hours at a time to protect themselves. Or ask one of the six hundred thousand coalition soldiers involved in Desert Shield how comfortable those M17 gas masks were, with the accompanying suits insulated with heavy charcoal.

Or, more to the point, ask the Kurdish relatives and friends who survived what their kin did not — Saddam Hussein's use of poison gas to kill five thousand Kurds in northern Iraq in 1988. The fear of gassing was one reason more than a million Kurds fled Iraq after Hussein survived the war. Or ask those who escaped the fate of the twenty thousand Iranians who died terrible deaths from Hussein's chemical-biological weapons in the Iraq-Iran war of the 1980s.

It is likely that President Bush was not fully aware of the price he and the American people would have to pay when he emphasized in a 1990 United Nations speech that a major goal of his was to obliterate chemical weapons from the earth. That goal was certainly tested as the United States spearheaded Desert Storm, in part to de-claw Iraq's military threat. Hussein's nuclear threat was still substantially in the future, but what contributed to his immediate potential for harm was his known stocks of chemical and biological weaponry and his willingness to use them.

As the Desert Shield buildup was escalating, the October 1, 1990, issue of *Time* published that Iraq already had "missiles being filled (not just) with chemical but with biological warheads. American experts believed that besides mustard and nerve gases, Iraqi warheads could spread powders that when inhaled cause anthrax and botulism, two diseases that can be fatal in two to three days." It was also reported that Iraq had missiles that could deliver deadly toxins up to nearly six hundred miles.

There are indications that the coalition attacks were so skillful and comprehensive that the Iraqis were in too much disarray to retaliate with chemical weapons. But even so, this does not diminish the enormity of what might have happened had the Iraqi madman not been stopped in his tracks. And until Saddam Hussein is deposed, he is a formidable force to be reckoned with.

Articles in *The New York Times* and elsewhere indicate that not only is Hussein stockpiling chemical weapons, but so are his neighbors — Syria, Israel, Iran, Egypt and Libya. In Libya Qaddafi has used chemical weapons in his war against Chad and found them so effective as a "weapon of mass destruction" that he's going all out, not only in a known factory, but in a huge underground plant about which little has been discovered, according to a White House spokesman quoted in *USA TODAY* on June 19, 1990.

The Soviets and the Americans are also making chemical weapons. The Soviets used "yellow rain" in Afghanistan. Bush announced that after a thirteen-year halt in production of chemical weapons in the 1970s and 1980s, $1 billion annually is being spent on their production.

More to Come

Sitting on one-eighth of the world's oil reserves, and with Iraq's nuclear and biological weapons production facilities still intact, Saddam Hussein is hardly down and out. As A.V. Brazys commented in *The Toronto Star* just after the war's end, perhaps Hussein is possessed with a demonic resolve that, having lost the battle, he'll yet win his war. *The Washington Post* observed that senior U.S. officials have concluded that Saddam Hussein's grip on power is stronger now than before Iraqi forces invaded Kuwait. He has decisively defeated the most serious internal threat to his regime since he became president of Iraq in 1979. Despite repeated predictions before and during the Gulf War that Saddam Hussein could not long survive a devastating military defeat, administration officials no longer regard his ouster as likely.

Even if Saddam Hussein is not the next figurehead to precipitate conflict in that arena, the simmering conflicts and the weaponry are in place to make the Gulf War look like a school-yard tussle. Not only has there been a proliferation of "smart bombs" and chemical weapons, but, as we'll see next, the potential for destruction by nuclear weapons on an Armageddon scale is greater than ever.

THREE

THE NUCLEAR THREAT

"FOR IN one hour is thy judgment come," wrote John regarding Babylon (Rev. 18:10). However, judgment would have come in a fraction of a second on twentieth-century Babylon if General Norman Schwarzkopf had had his way.

Schwarzkopf sought permission from President Bush to explode a high-tech, nuclear-class weapon high over Iraq, according to the January 14, 1991, *Newsweek*. The president turned him down. But the existence of this weapon, as well as many traditional nuclear warheads, shows that the use of nuclear weapons is by no means restricted to a global-scale, superpower confrontation. Even a regional conflict involving a nation as tiny as Kuwait has the potential for leading to events that would fulfill all the Bible's prophecies regarding the unthinkable war of Armageddon.

Checking the Pulse

What was this super weapon that the spunky general wanted to use? It's called an electromagnetic pulse device. The December 10, 1990, issue of *Time* described it as "an 'electronic blanket' suffocating all communications between enemy headquarters and their troops in the field." It would have accomplished in one-billionth of a second what it apparently took thousands of conventional bombs to achieve.

The Toronto Star, quoting from the German newspaper *Die Zeit* in February 1991, described how such a bomb would be capable of crippling all electronic systems in the United States. Imagine a satellite, allegedly on a routine mission, crossing over the United States at a height of 450 kilometers. Suddenly over the Great Plains a few pounds of enriched plutonium in the fake satellite explodes, blanketing the United States and Canada with a shower of gamma rays. In one-billionth of a second all electrical power and transmissions in North America are blanked out. Cars, trucks and machinery stop. Nuclear power plants go dark. Radio and television stations go off the air. Planes crash. Missile systems fail, and the president of the United States has no way to communicate with the silo crews and set the missiles off on a retaliatory strike. This effect is called a Nuclear Electro-Magnetic Pulse, and even in an age of increasingly horrifying weapons it is giving the Pentagon and NATO nightmares.

Die Zeit devoted two pages to a description of this "satanic weapon that can cripple the total nervous system of civilization." The article says that "scientific and military journals are paying more and more attention to a doomsday scenario that begins with a Nuclear Electro-Magnetic Pulse."

Iraq's Nuclear Threat

During the Gulf War, prominent commentators such as Richard Gwyn of London believed the main reasons the United States led the United Nations coalition forces into

Desert Storm were the defense of Israel and the security of oil. Yet the American people, responding in a Gallup poll, believed the primary reason was to stop Saddam Hussein before he was able to develop a nuclear bomb to intimidate his neighbors into subordination.

President Bush felt that if Hussein was given time to perfect his nuclear intentions, it might spell Armageddon, beginning with a nuclear strike on Israel. As the decision to follow Desert Shield with Desert Storm was being made, Bush said, "An unchecked aggression today would lead to some horrible world conflagration tomorrow."

If the American people judged correctly that Desert Storm was mounted primarily to stop Hussein from triggering a nuclear war, there was clearly a compelling, though perhaps understated, fear of worldwide nuclear holocaust. And with good reason: *The Bible implies a Middle East war will be the next to the last step toward Armageddon.*

Just how real was this worry over Iraq's nuclear potential? *The New York Times* on January 21, 1991, described how Iraq had three nuclear reactor sites and at least four nuclear research laboratories. It was the announced intent of the coalition bombing missions of early 1991 to destroy these installations. They were apparently only damaged, and the continuing efforts of the United Nations — led by the United States — demonstrate that, contrary to world opinion at the conclusion of Desert Storm, Saddam Hussein was not stopped in his tracks.

Israel's Nuclear Arsenal

Because Israel, with Jerusalem at its center (see Luke 21:20, 24), is to play such an integral part during the seven years leading up to Armageddon, and because it appears that nuclear weapons will play a major role in that apocalyptical scenario, it's vitally important to understand Israel's nuclear capabilities.

Arabs contend: Israel has the bomb, so why shouldn't we? Israel has never officially admitted to having nuclear bombs. The reason may be that to do so would weaken its security and its bargaining posture. The truth is that Israel has probably had them for twenty-five years, at least since the war in 1967 when it took over the West Bank, including all of Jerusalem. I remember when I was in Jerusalem in late 1967. A Jewish government official with whom I was staying told me that even then Israel had nuclear bombs ready to use at a moment's notice.

In 1972, during the Yom Kippur War, the very existence of Israel was threatened, and President Nixon called for an international alert. The Soviets — to be followed by the Arab nations — backed away. The media reported widely that Israel had thirteen nuclear bombs emplaned on military runways. They were never used. The final countdown to Armageddon had not yet begun, at least visibly. But the clock was ticking.

Once again, in 1982, the Israeli nuclear forces were on high alert. This was when the Israelis charged into Lebanon, and the Soviets, through their client states — especially Syria — came close to making a decision to invade Israel.

Since then it has come to light that Israel has a massive top-secret nuclear weapons plant at Dimona, deep in the Negev Desert. Saddam Hussein aimed and fired two Scud missiles in an effort to hit Dimona, but the Israeli military said nothing about it. Despite a constant stream of reports by foreign experts about Israel's nuclear capability, Israel has steadfastly refused to acknowledge it has any atomic weapons.

One Israeli, however, has been willing to talk. In 1986 a former nuclear technician at the Dimona plant, Mordecai Vanunu, revealed in striking detail the extent of Israel's nuclear weaponry. His story appeared in *The Sunday Times* of London and was reprinted in Israeli newspapers. Vanunu later was seized by Israeli agents, spirited out of Britain back to Israel and sentenced to eighteen years in an Israeli prison on three counts of treason and espionage.

Those who knew Vanunu contend that he revealed what he knew to *The Sunday Times* in order to warn the world that Armageddon was closer than most people thought. Israeli officials have never denied Vanunu's story.

The *Times* article concludes, "Far from being a nuclear pygmy, the evidence is that Israel must now be regarded as a major power." The nation is believed to have two hundred nuclear weapons and is thought to be making neutron and hydrogen bombs as well, turning out a new bomb every thirty-seven days.

Frank Barnaby, writing in his book *The Invisible Bomb: The Nuclear Arms Race in the Middle East*, confirms not only that Israel has a minimum of two hundred nuclear weapons, but estimates they also have about thirty-five much more powerful thermonuclear bombs.

The *Sunday Times* article says that Israel has thermonuclear weapons powerful enough to destroy entire cities. Indeed, the Israelis leaked to the media early in 1991 that they would not hesitate to turn Baghdad into a sea of molten glass if Saddam Hussein were to detonate a chemical or biological bomb in a populated area of Israel. Israel has a history of delivering first, talking later. This leak to the media may well have been why Hussein did not front-load any of his Scuds with anything other than conventional bombs. He foresaw the consequences accurately.

Even if Israel is well-equipped with nuclear devices,

one may ask, Can these lethal devices be delivered to their desired destinations? They can. The *Sunday Times* article states that Israel has the missiles to carry nuclear warheads two thousand kilometers (1,243 miles) to their directed targets.

Perhaps the most convincing signal Israel has sent regarding its ability to deliver a nuclear punch took place in the spring of 1990. The day after Saddam Hussein boasted before the international community, "By God, we will make the fire eat up half of Israel if it tries to do anything against Iraq," an Israeli Jericho 2 missile put a satellite into orbit. This missile could just as easily place a nuclear warhead over Baghdad.

Global Nuclear Capabilities

What about the nuclear capacity of other nations around the world? According to the February 19, 1991, edition of *The Toronto Star*, the Soviet Union has twenty-seven thousand nuclear weapons; the United States (for official purposes), the same number; Great Britain has seven hundred; France, five hundred; and China, three hundred.

Then there is the matter of small countries getting nuclear bombs, which a June 3, 1985, issue of *Time* took seriously: "Nuclear proliferation (on the part of Third World nations) makes the superpower arms race look like a comparatively minor league problem." And again in *Time*, "What about all those Third World countries that will soon have nuclear capability? They have so little to lose, and our large cities make such wonderful targets."

One study concluded that forty-four countries had the capability to detonate a nuclear device. A March 21, 1991, *Toronto Star* report warned that fifteen developing countries were putting in place their own ballistic missiles, while six of them were getting ready to acquire intermediate-range ballistic missiles, each one capable of carrying nuclear bombs to their preprogrammed targets. It may seem impossible for Third World countries to obtain such sophisticated weapons of mass destruction, but it is not. Countries who are rich from oil have a great capacity to buy these weapons in the very active black market.

Special Delivery

As signs of a foreseeable Armageddon become more and more apparent, it is important to note that a proliferation of nuclear weapons alone cannot wreak the havoc revealed in biblical prophecy. They need means of being delivered to their intended destinations in order to effect such apocalyptical destruction.

The American defense system is a pattern used by several nations for how nuclear bombs are deployed. It is based on a land-air-sea triad. Land-based nuclear weapons are in a worldwide network of silos dug into the ground. Weapons are classified as short-range, medium-range and intercontinental. They are guarded with maximum security, precisely programmed with guidance systems, constantly maintained and kept on alert.

Then there are the heavy bombers deployed to U.S. strategic bases throughout the world. They also are kept on alert, loaded with nuclear bombs.

Third, there are the nuclear submarines. They circle the oceans and seas, poised at all times to unleash a nuclear holocaust on determined targets. The United States has approximately one-third of its total nuclear bombs aboard submarines. A U.S. Poseidon submarine is equipped with sixteen missiles, each with ten warheads, which could destroy 160 targets. The larger Trident submarine is capable of destroying 500 targets.

The Soviets, even back in the eighties, had three times as many submarines as the United States. But what is most ominous is that, according to *The Los Angeles Times*, they have titanic nuclear submarines — behemoths nearly as big as the American Essex-class aircraft carrier, with displacement of thirty thousand tons. Experts say one Soviet submarine carries sufficient nuclear bombs to wipe out two hundred million Americans and is capable of delivering them with pinpoint accuracy. Christian author Hal Lindsey, who has done a good deal of research into this theme, claims that despite all the propaganda to the contrary, the Soviet nuclear strike capacity remains substantially superior to that of the United States, especially in the sphere of submarine capability.

Accidents

These vast webs of advanced weaponry pose danger enough, considering mankind's proclivity toward war. How much worse, then, when we consider another common trait of man: goofing up.

The May 26, 1981, *New York Times* warned that there have been thirty-two serious nuclear weapon accidents, according to Pentagon admissions. These could have killed millions of people if they hadn't been reversed in the nick of time. The *Times* stated that the Center for Defense Information in Washington, D.C., insists there have been at least ninety-six such accidents.

I was staying near Cambridge, England, one time when a B-47 bomber crashed into a nuclear bomb storage center. Nuclear detonation eighteen hundred times that of Hiroshima was prevented by an incredible "miracle." It was estimated that twenty million people would have died. Much of eastern England would have become a desert.

An even closer call occurred when a crashing B-52 bomber released its cargo of two nuclear bombs over Goldsboro, North Carolina. One broke apart on impact. The other, floating down on a parachute, was caught in a tree. As it drifted down, five of the six safety switches were released. Only one switch prevented the explosion of a 24-megaton bomb, eighteen hundred times more powerful than the one dropped on Hiroshima.

Then there is the possibility of computer error. An article in *The Toronto Star* told how the Union of Concerned Scientists warned that for the second time in seven months a computer at the nation's missile warning center erroneously put U.S. strategic forces on alert against an (alien) missile attack on the United States, according to Pentagon sources. Overdependence on computer warning systems for nuclear weapons could possibly lead to a real nuclear war.

Or how about the Soviet nuclear submarine that beached on a Swedish shore? The Swedes, a levelheaded people, did not overreact. But what would happen if that had occurred on the shore of a country which read such an event as an act of war? Or what if, in the beaching, a nuclear bomb had been triggered and detonated?

The odds are that accidents will eventually result in something other than a narrow escape (if intentional war does not transpire first). As the June 11, 1984, issue of *Time* puts it, the world's fifty thousand nuclear weapons have reached "critical mass. Just one of those bombs going off could touch off a chain reaction leading to the extinction of the human race.... [Scientists and politicians] continue to proliferate and refine their offensive weapons. In so doing, they put arsenals on hair trigger; the danger grows that in a crisis or an accident, one or both fingers could twitch."

Reading such accounts in the press should cause people to turn to biblical prophecies of the last days, such as those found in Joel: "A fire devoureth before them; and behind them a flame burneth...[into] desolate wilderness; yea, and nothing shall escape" (2:3); or "The fire hath devoured the pastures of the wilderness, and the flame hath burned all the trees of the field" (1:19). Isaiah foretells that "the inhabitants of the earth are burned, and few men left" (24:6).

After viewing the worldwide television broadcast of the Gulf War, only those who stick their heads in the sand can remain ignorant of the capacity for destruction that mere conventional weapons have. However, comparing what happened in early 1991 to what nuclear war will be like leading to Armageddon is like comparing a burning match to a blowtorch.

FOUR

DOOM IN EVERY CORNER

DON'T CALL the 415-673-DOOM recorded message in San Francisco if you need a little lift. Typical of what you may hear is a mournful tolling of bells followed by a sober voice stating: "Doom is the Society for Secular Armageddonism — an array of threats are combining to bring the earth to the brink of apocalypse...contrary to conventional wisdom, the end of the world is...at hand." According to the news accounts of the 1990s, the recorded message says the earth is doomed because of nuclear proliferation, chemical/biological weapons, deforestation, AIDS, global warming, ozone depletion, acid rain, the poisoning of our air and waters, rising racism, massive species loss, global famine, rampant greed, toxic waste, exploding population, encroaching Big Brotherness, worldwide complacency and another one thousand points of blight.

"These are grade A, unadulterated harbingers of destruction, 100 percent bona fide specters of doom, and they prove we don't need God to finish it for us," said the message. "The coming will be strictly do-it-yourself apocalypse."

Gloomy enough? You can write this off as yet another

nut fringe on the West Coast. But the fact is Armageddon awareness is spreading, and it's certainly not limited to the religious community.

Take Isaac Asimov, for example, a noted secular humanist and probably the world's most credible and widely read science writer. His bestseller *A Choice of Catastrophies* lists a range of possibilities as to how man (without an intervention from God) can do himself in. He believes that, one way or another, it will happen.

As Christians we believe God has a clear plan for Armageddon and its preliminary events. However, it should come as no surprise if God utilizes the very creations and circumstances we see around us to bring about His ends. So before leaving this discussion of modern armaments, let's scan some other trends, exotic weaponry and the growing world bazaar for their sale. These machines and their spread make it clear Armageddon could come very soon.

A Nuclear Cover-up

Perhaps the scariest news since Desert Storm has been the stories issuing from Chernobyl five years after that disastrous nuclear meltdown. The May 19, 1986, issue of *Time* reported how Chernobyl was "like a biblical calamity...felt everywhere." The world, however, discredited reports such as one in the May 2, 1986, *New York Post* with the headline "MASS GRAVE FOR 15,000 VICTIMS." The story claimed that fifteen thousand bodies were being buried in a mass grave at a nuclear waste site southwest of Chernobyl. The corpses allegedly were "being carried in convoys of Soviet military vehicles, seen rumbling along the small backroads by residents of the vicinity." The international community preferred the Soviet government version, numbering the dead at thirty-one.

However, Vladimir Chernousenko, the scientist who was in charge of the surrounding zone when the accident occurred, decided to tell the world the truth when in 1991 he was dying from the exposure he had to the lethal radiation. He estimated the numbers were perhaps ten thousand, not the official thirty-one. Mikhail Gorbachev himself conceded as much when he appealed for international assistance in the light of thousands more who were still dying, reinforcing his views during the autumn of 1991 by letting it be known that two decades before Chernobyl there had been a much worse nuclear accident which had been skillfully concealed from the rest of the world.

One of the effects of Chernousenko's revelation about Chernobyl was reflected in an Associated Press story distributed in April 1991 saying that Chernobyl had renewed fear of nuclear war. In the early 1980s there were terrifying fears of nuclear war which then diminished. But now they're back! Consequently, we do well to consider what the concerned nuclear scientists are saying about the future.

Missing People

Prophetic Scripture speaks of fire at the end time. One such source that may fulfill these prophecies — completely unknown to the scientific community previous to the latter twentieth century — is the neutron bomb. *The New York Times* of August 9, 1981, noted these bombs are "designed to produce far more radiation and far less blast and heat than other tactical nuclear weapons, so that they kill people without severe damage to their surroundings." Some scientists have observed that Zechariah 14:12 describes the effects of the neutron bomb: "Their flesh shall consume away while they stand...and their tongue shall consume away in their mouth."

The June 12, 1981, *Toronto Globe and Mail* notes that the decision to go ahead with the neutron bomb was the biggest step taken toward Armageddon since 1961. The United States, France and Israel are among those nations known to possess the bomb.

Carl Sagan, celebrated for his "Cosmos" television series, calculates that it would take only one hundred nuclear bombs to plunge the Northern Hemisphere into nuclear winter, resulting in the death of a third of the human race, prevailing darkness and a drop of temperatures by as much as seventy degrees. The most powerful hydrogen bomb could produce heat of 150 million degrees Fahrenheit and in one-millionth of a second unleash more destructive energy than all the wars of history combined.

Volkmar Deile, a German, was quoted in *Time* (October 19, 1982) as reasoning that "there is an increasing feeling that like drug addicts" the nations today "are hooked" on nuclear death weaponry. His sentiment was echoed by Helen Caldicott, a Harvard professor of medicine who described ours as a "terminally ill planet" when she addressed the World Council of Churches in Vancouver in 1983. She remonstrated that "international politicians are like nine-year-old boys in a sandbox, [only] they are building nuclear warheads, rather than sand castles, and are setting the stage for a battle that could kill hundreds of millions of people in its first hour.... Millions more would die of radiation illness, starvation, uncontrolled epidemics and burns. Winds traveling hundreds of kilometers an hour would turn people into human missiles."

Star Wars Reborn

Not only is our defense network utilizing the land-sea-air triad, but we are drawing closer to the military use of outer space. In the mid-1980s President Reagan launched his Strategic Defense Initiative program, popularly known as Star Wars. It envisages launching hundreds of large satellites into orbit with particle beams, homing rockets and massive lasers attached.

Lasers can be used to perform high-precision surgical operations on the body to save lives. Or they can be mounted on jets or satellites, capable in combat of knocking airplanes from the sky or knocking missiles with nuclear warheads from space — as far as five thousand miles away — if the technology can be developed sufficiently.

Circling the earth in their orbiting trajectories under the SDI proposal, satellites would be fitted with monitoring devices, scanning the earth in search of any nuclear intercontinental ballistic missiles rising from enemy silos. Spotting one, the first of these weapons to pick up the signal would lock in on its target and either zap it with a laser or particle beam or else fire a rocket to destroy it. Killer satellites are capable of destroying several orbiting enemy satellites. The idea is to have antisatellite battle stations equipped with clusters of infrared homing-guided interceptors that could destroy multiple enemy spacecraft.

Watching the Patriot missiles demolish the Iraqi-launched Scud missiles on CNN during Desert Storm, the public learned, on a small scale, how such an idea functions. In fact, whereas before the war it was thought by many that the Star Wars program was unworkable, and even if workable, too impractical and costly, now it's been revived. Projections in 1991 called for beginning full

45

production of the system in 1993. *The New York Times*, on April 3, 1991, reported that the Pentagon is secretly "developing a nuclear-powered rocket for hauling [these] giant weapons and other military payloads into space as part of the 'Star Wars' program."

So how do these developments relate to arming for Armageddon? Revelation 12:7 speaks of "war in heaven." Revelation 13:13 says the Antichrist would cause "great wonders, so that he maketh fire come down from heaven on the earth in the sight of men." Star Wars technology may well be a partial fulfillment of such a prophecy.

Peace: An Endangered Species

William F. Buckley, like many conservatives, believes the best recipe for peace is to prepare for war. Of course, many others disagree completely. If Buckley is correct, the world is going in the right direction. There are now four tons of explosives for every man, woman and child in the world. The Worldwatch Institute in Washington reckons that the annual expenditure on armaments is $1 trillion and growing rapidly in the wake of the Gulf War.

After the dazzling display of weaponry in Desert Storm, virtually every nation on earth is eager to get in on the military action. As columnist Mike Royko of *The Chicago Tribune* puts it, the war was "one of the biggest and most successful trade shows in human history." The presentation of fancy new war gadgets on worldwide television — "all those roaring jets, fast-moving tanks, muscular helicopters, intellectual missiles, and night vision goggles — was viewed by the rulers and generals in other countries as a terrific TV commercial for our high-tech weapons industry."

The Vietnam War news imagery left the public dazed and horrified as the sickening scenes of killing dragged on year after year. Desert Storm left most people dazzled and, on the part of hundreds of millions, applauding for the sequel. Man's inhumanity to man has never been so mesmerizing, which makes Armageddon seem that much more inevitable.

A Thriving Death Business

Armaments had never been such big business worldwide as they were in 1991. This was a complete contrast to early 1990 when peace lobbies had portrayed arms makers and merchants as grossly immoral or savage people.

The Wall Street Journal reported on March 5, 1991, that, thanks to the Gulf War, American defense contractors were "salivating" at the prospect of selling a wide range of death-and-destruction gadgetry to countries in the Middle East and elsewhere. Of course, the United States could take the moral high ground and say, "No, we will not help any of you short-tempered nations build bigger and nastier armies and air forces so you can go back at it again." But as the *Journal* indicated, the U.S. business community will be unlikely to get carried away by such morality. One reason is that European arms makers would nullify such good intentions by meeting the demand for weapons.

And who needs business more than the Soviet Union — or China, or Brazil, or Israel, or South Africa, or Canada? My homeland of Canada, which purports to be a peacekeeping nation, has upped its defense budget to $19.5 billion. Peter Goodspeed commented in *The Toronto Star* of April 5, 1991, "Shocked by the killing power of American hi-tech weapons during the Persian Gulf War, China is launching a massive new arms-building program that could have dramatic repercussions in

Asia and the Third World." Will China be a part of Armageddon? A glance at the Living Bible's Revelation 9:16 footnotes indicates it could be.

With all of the reports of economic woe coming out of the Soviet Union, it could easily be overlooked that the Soviets have an 11 percent heftier chunk of the total armaments-selling market than the United States. They are masters of espionage and masters at copying technology the West has labored long and hard to invent and perfect. So it can be assumed that one of their biggest undertakings now is to duplicate the high-tech equipment the Americans introduced in such spectacular display in Desert Storm. All of this could well be what Ezekiel 38:4 prophesies — that when the Russian-led armies charge with their coalition forces on Israel, they'll be equipped with "all sorts of armour."

Libya, Ethiopia and Persia (Iran/Iraq) are noted in the next verse (Ezek. 38:5) as part of that coalition that attacks Israel. Ethiopia, despite its tragic poverty and famine, has the largest army in Africa. The nation has spent billions of dollars on its military force — as well as received billions of dollars' worth of armaments from the Soviets.

With billions of dollars' worth of Soviet-built weaponry already in its possession, Libya is going all out to arm itself even further. Libya's Mu'ammar Qaddafi is probably correct when he says that Israel has missiles with nuclear warheads pointed at every one of the Arab capitals, so he is pushing relentlessly to develop nuclear weapons and other means of mass destruction.

Reports are that the postwar Saddam Hussein is more dominant over Iraq than he's ever been. Iraq is reportedly salvaging what it can and regrouping to rebuild its power. CNN News reported on April 29, 1991, that Hussein held his best leaders and troops out of Desert Storm. As a dependent of the Soviets, he stands to gain back his losses from that relationship.

As for the other half of biblical Persia — Iran — a former U.S. ambassador to Iran, Charles Floweree, says that's who he'd pick as the war's Mideast winner, along with Islamic fundamentalism. Armageddon is rendered even more likely as "the Sword of Islam" becomes increasingly unsheathed against an Israel which is boosting its military might with every passing day. Israel "has just finished a second round of testing Arrow anti-ballistic missiles that 'leave the Patriot in the stone age of weaponry,' " according to *The Toronto Star* of April 15, 1991. For Israel, with its brainpower and level of scientific education so far above other nations on a per capita basis, "high technology is the way of the future. The Gulf War proved decisively brain will win over brawn in the military field, as far as the eye can see."

So it may be justifiably thought that far more consequential than Desert Storm itself, in terms of moving man toward Armageddon, is the current explosion in arms production. *New York Times* columnist Tom Wicker observed, "Wouldn't it be ironic if the defeat of Iraq resulted in a Third World newly armed to the teeth with smart bombs, ballistic and cruise missiles, helicopter gunships, Patriot-styled interceptors and radar-invisible aircraft? That would make wars between Third World rivals more likely, if one nation thought it had gained a qualitative advantage over another." Not only would these wars be more destructive, but industrialized nations would also be more likely to get involved to guard their interests and promote their weaponry.

Wicker wrote that "the Bush administration has informed Congress that it wants to sell high-tech weapons worth $18 billion...to five Persian Gulf allies. With such weapons going to Arab nations, Israel's defense worries are bound to increase."

Can We Truly Disarm?

In light of what is going on in the early 1990s as contrasted to what was happening during the late 1980s, disarmament treaties seem to be exercises in futility and hypocrisy.

As President Reagan said many times, once arms are manufactured and put in place, history shows they have always been used. Speaking before the joint Houses of Parliament in England in 1982, he lamented, "In today's world, the existence of nuclear weapons could mean, if not the extinction of mankind, then surely the end of civilization as we know it." His Canadian counterpart, Pierre Trudeau, was equally clear on the imperative that "disarmament is no less than the survival of humanity on this planet."

The hope of reaching international agreements to ban chemical and biological weapons is also dim. The United States and the Soviet Union reached verbal agreement in 1990 to eliminate most of their chemical weapons in eleven years. But a Reuters news report of March 8, 1991, indicated those preliminary arrangements have lapsed. Whatever the well-meaning peace advocates of the world may think and do, the arms race, be it chemical or nuclear, is not going to shrink prior to Armageddon.

Harvey Cox of Harvard University reflected in *The Toronto Star* on April 10, 1982, how a visit to Hiroshima changed his life: "Standing at the Centopath there, I felt rooted, paralyzed, unable to leave. What had before been just a mental awareness of the bomb, hit me in my chromosomes. I realized this was the post where everything had changed. I knew in my innermost self that Hiroshima was the first step towards a capability to annihilate the species and the earth itself."

Kenneth Kantzer challenged evangelicals in *Christi-*

anity Today when he said it's just a matter of time before the day when "someone will push the button that will set off a chain reaction among nations. As each seeks to defend his allies, the whole world will go up in flames. Does the Christian faith have anything to say about this?"

Indeed it does!

Jesus prophesied the present predicament but also prescribed a remedy: "There will be strange events in the skies — warnings, evil omens and portents in the sun, moon and stars; and down here on earth the nations will be in turmoil, perplexed.... The courage of many people will falter because of the fearful fate they see coming upon the earth.... Then the peoples of the earth shall see me, the Messiah, coming in a cloud with power and great glory. So when all these things begin to happen, stand straight and look up! For your salvation is near" (Luke 21:25-28, TLB).

In such promises we can take hope. Though God's ordained plan for history cannot be altered, He has revealed enough for His people to stand above those whose courage will falter in such days. Those belonging to Christ can stand and look confidently as their final redemption draws nigh.

FIVE

"FROM ONE END OF HEAVEN TO THE OTHER"

"WE'RE NOT too far from going to the stars," exclaimed Commander John Young, emerging from the $10 billion space shuttle Columbia.

His optimism is hardly without company. Morris Sneiderman predicted at the Washington Conference of the American Association for the Advancement of Science that the permanent establishment of communities and factories in space would take place in his lifetime. "The era of tentative probing is over," he said. Billy Graham has said he expects there soon will be "food factories orbiting in outer space."

Do such developments relate to Christ's second coming? I believe they do, particularly to the second phase of His return. "Immediately after the tribulation of those days (that is, Armageddon)...he shall send his angels with a great sound of a trumpet, and they shall gather together his elect from the four winds, from one end of heaven to the other" (Matt. 24:29,31).

Jesus did not say from one end of the earth to the other. He said *from one end of heaven to the other*. We no longer need to discount terms such as "heaven" as grandiose versions of what fits our earthly perspective. As we will see in this chapter, advances in space exploration and our knowledge of the universe are showing that God's prophetic Word can be taken quite literally. And it appears that its fulfillment is quite imminent.

Space Colonies

Science fiction writer Isaac Asimov has predicted human colonization of other worlds, starting with the moon, so that people can escape "catastrophies." The Bible has another name for what Asimov sees man escaping from: Armageddon. Asimov expects that within a century fifty thousand people will live in a "luna city" on the moon. While earthlings threaten to exterminate each other, he projects that lunarians will set up a new civilization.

Asimov is a writer, but U.S. and Soviet space scientists are doers. A Reuters report indicates they are preparing to launch the world's first permanent space village, housing one hundred cosmonauts. The United States has long talked of manned space stations.

There is also a dark side to these glowing advancements. U.S. sources claim the Soviet space stations, with a continuous human presence, would serve "as a base for an anti-ballistic missile laser weapon." *The Los Angeles Times* reports that the Soviets have tested "the world's first fighter spacecraft," a delta-winged vehicle capable of carrying people to a space station on a military mission. In other words, these forays into space may play a key role in Armageddon.

It is an alarming reality, observed Daniel Deudne, researcher for Worldwatch Institute in Washington, D.C., that "the two superpowers today spend 15 percent or more of their space research funds on military activities." They're actually spending much more to promote death on earth than life in space.

Emerging Signs

Jesus said, "There shall be signs in the sun, and in the moon, and in the stars...for the powers of heaven shall be shaken. And then shall they see the Son of man coming in a cloud with power and great glory" (Luke 21:25-27).

The Jewish Chronicle reports that a team of experts is working on a project to place giant aluminum mirrors on the moon. These, says the *Chronicle*, would be used for lighting at night and to provide a vast savings in electricity and power. This could perhaps qualify as an end-times sign on the moon. Some have even speculated that such a development, perhaps attacked during Armageddon, might tie into Jesus' prophecy: "After that tribulation...the moon shall not give her light" (Mark 13:24).

The prophet Daniel (12:4) foresaw at "the time of the end" that "many shall run to and fro." This could be translated loosely as moving at incredible speeds over vast distances.

In the 1990s passengers cross the Atlantic at 1,500 miles per hour in the Concorde. Astronauts have gone to the moon and back at 25,000 miles per hour. The United States and the Soviet Union have talked about sending people to Mars. And there are Pioneer X and Explorer III, which travel three billion miles from earth — soaring out of the solar system with nearly all of their equipment functioning. These things which we have begun to accept as ordinary may be evidences, according to Daniel 12:4, that the end times have drawn near.

The Heavens Declare the Glory

United Press International reports that British and Australian scientists have discovered through use of the world's most sophisticated telescope the quasar PKS-

2000-330. Because this quasar — a celestial object that emits light and radio waves — is eighteen billion light years from earth, it provides possible evidence that the universe had an explosive origin about that long ago and that this quasar may be at the outer edge of the universe.

"Our universe could have been created by God," wrote physicist Heinz Pagels, of Rockefeller University, in *The New York Times*. Pagels, author of *The Cosmic Code: Quantum Physics as the Language of Nature*, reached this conclusion based on the broad agreement among physicists that the universe began with a big-bang explosion. He went on to say in the *Times*: "Not so long ago, this remarkable creation story was unknown. But in the last two decades, scientists have learned more about the origin of the universe than in previous centuries — a consequence of two major developments." Those developments were improved technology for space exploration and unified field theories of sub-nuclear quantum particles. Pagels observed that understanding the laws that govern the smallest things — quantum particles — helps physicists to reconstruct the origin of the largest thing — the entire universe.

This also was the view of perhaps the world's most credible astrophysicist, the late Fred Hoyle of Cambridge, who coined the term "big bang" and gave credence to the theory. Hoyle was converted from agnosticism to theism by what he concluded was the scientific evidence for such a basic belief.

So what relevance has the big bang to the second coming of Christ, to Armageddon and to "the end of all things" (1 Pet. 4:7)? It is a widely held assumption among astrophysicists that, as the big bang giveth, the big bang taketh away. That is, physical creation will go out of existence with another big bang. Second Peter 3:10 reveals that "the day of the Lord will come as a thief in the night; in the which the heavens shall pass away with a great noise," to be replaced by "new heavens and a new earth" (v. 13).

The Big Squeeze

You may remember visiting the circus as a child and wondering how twenty big clowns could get out of one small car — and then get back in again. But it happened. Seeing was believing.

Compression of much greater magnitude takes place in the universe. Unlike the clown trick, we cannot see it firsthand. But we can believe it. And like so many other scientific discoveries, it reveals the vast and eternal purposes of God in His plan for His creation.

Scientist Terence Dickinson has explored the phenomenon of black holes — collections of matter in outer space whose density is so great that even light rays cannot escape their gravity. Based on the physics of black holes, Dickinson has concluded that earth could be compressed into the size of a grape. For laymen, such mind-bending theorizing is beyond comprehension. Yet this is a hint of what God has in store for His conclusion to physical reality. "And all the host of heaven shall be dissolved, and the heavens shall be rolled together as a scroll" (Is. 34:4). Scientists are explaining — wittingly or unwittingly — what God can do when it comes time for Him to pronounce "The End."

Preparing for Eternity

Bible scholar C.I. Scofield wrote ninety years ago, "Nothing brings us into such molding intimacy with God as the believing study of prophecy." And nothing, I must add, makes us so earthly good for heaven's sake. With the second coming of Christ to look forward to, what stronger motivation to live constructively do we need? To be heaven-born is to be heaven-bound. As Thomas Carlyle, a nineteenth century philosopher, exhorted, to have a true vision of eternity is to get a true hold of time.

No space shot is ever made without arduous and meticulous preparation. Even then accidents sometimes occur, such as the explosion of the Challenger space shuttle.

How do we prepare for our spiritual voyage to heaven? How can we be ready for Christ's coming? Scripture tells us, "Prepare to meet thy God" (Amos 4:12) and "prepare ye the way of the Lord" (Luke 3:4). We do this by repenting of our sins and trusting in Jesus Christ as Lord.

A space scientist said on television's "Meet the Press" that man can achieve "infinity in space and eternity in time." With Jesus, we're assured that time and eternity eventually will be one, and we'll go to the farthest reaches of infinity in space by a fulfilled faith in Christ as Lord.

When I'm planning to leave Toronto for the United States, I make reservations and purchase my ticket. Then on the day of the flight I just show up and get on the plane, a seat having been reserved for me in advance. Have you called on Jesus Christ for your spiritual reservations? He assures us, "Whosoever shall call upon the name of the Lord shall be saved" (Rom. 10:13).

Jesus says, "Him that cometh to me I will in no wise cast out" (John 6:37). He never rejects those who come to God by Him. He takes you all the way through life, with its often bumpy passage, and into eternity, forever to be with the Lord.

Astronaut Neil Armstrong insists he did not say when he strode out onto the moon — as is commonly believed — "That's one small step for man, one giant leap for mankind." What he did say was, "That's one small step for *a* man, one giant leap for mankind." Likewise, each of us must take the initial step *individually* for Christ if we would one day go to be with the Lord forever. Church membership will not guarantee your reservation. It's the personal decision made from the heart that God will honor.

What we do know is that when Jesus Christ comes again, He is going to take us to be with Himself eternally — at which time He will issue to us new, glorified, celestial bodies. The astronauts were able to go to the moon and back because they wore space suits which had been tailored according to long-studied and precise specifications so they would operate without the slightest malfunction. Then, and only then, could they rocket at the speed of 25,000 miles per hour to a distance of 250,000 miles from the earth and, after walking around heaven — in that the moon is a part of the "second heaven" — return safely to earth.

Wrote Paul to the Philippians, "Our [citizenship] is in heaven; from whence also we look for the Saviour, the Lord Jesus Christ: who shall change our vile body, that it may be fashioned like unto his glorious body, according to the working whereby he is able even to subdue all things unto himself" (Phil. 3:20-21).

We won't just put space suits on our mortal bodies. We'll be issued immortal bodies. Our terrestrial bodies will be "dissolved" (2 Cor. 5:1), and we'll be issued celestial ones. "We know that if our earthly house of this tabernacle were dissolved, we have a building of God, an house not made with hands, eternal in the heavens. For in this we [do] groan, earnestly desiring to be clothed upon with our house which is from heaven: if so be that being clothed we shall not be found naked" (2 Cor. 5:1-3).

So how will it happen? Paul explained, "Behold, I shew you a mystery; We shall not all sleep, but we shall all be changed, in a moment, in the twinkling of an eye, at the last trump: for the trumpet shall sound, and the dead shall be raised incorruptible, and we shall be changed. For this corruptible must put on incorruption, and this mortal must put on immortality. So when this corruptible shall have put on incorruption, and this mortal shall have put on immortality, then shall be brought to pass the saying that is written, Death is swallowed up in victory" (1 Cor. 15:51-54).

SIX

The Witness of Science

THOSE WHO routinely failed science courses need not worry about getting bogged down with theorems and technical concepts as they study Scripture. The word "science" appears only once in the King James translation of the Old Testament and once in the New Testament.

The Old Testament reference is in the book of Daniel. Young Jewish scholars, like Daniel, who served in the court of Nebuchadnezzar were "skillful in...understanding science" (Dan. 1:4). Though science had a much more restricted meaning then than it does today, we still can assume that Daniel was well-versed in the current knowledge of the world, as well as being a prophet. Yet Daniel insisted the knowledge of his day was primitive compared to what would happen at "the time of the end" when "knowledge shall be increased" (Dan. 12:4); or, as it may more literally be translated, "There will be a knowledge explosion."

In the New Testament the word "science" appears in Paul's writings to Timothy (1 Tim. 6:20), and it's in those same letters that he prophesies, "This know also, that in the last days" people will be "ever learning, and never able to come to the knowledge of the truth" (2 Tim. 3:1,7).

This chapter will look at the proliferation of knowledge, while the next will examine how that knowledge still does not bring anyone closer to the truth embodied in God, as revealed through Jesus Christ.

Scientists and scholars have been with us since God created man. Yet the prophetic Word makes clear that the end times will be marked by an acceleration of knowledge and knowledge-seekers. Sadly, as Paul predicted, many of them will never apprehend the most important purpose of knowledge: the saving grace of Jesus Christ. We will see in this chapter how the information explosion (much of it relating to war) taking place in our midst is another sure sign that God's plan for history is nearing its climax.

At What Price Knowledge?

Previous chapters have shown how man talks peace while he walks with ever-more-loaded arms, pointing to Armageddon. It's one of the monumental ironies of the 1990s that the Soviet Union, unable to provide adequately for the basic needs of its people, has excelled technologically in developing and manufacturing armaments. We're quite aware of how the Bible prophesies that our swords will be turned into plowshares and our spears into pruning hooks. But we tend to overlook Joel's prophecy that in the approach to the last days nations will "beat your plowshares into swords, and your pruninghooks into spears" (Joel 3:10). It's happening on a tragic scale today. Out of one side of their mouths many world leaders are saying, "Peace, peace," while out of the other side they say, "Make war! Make war!"

Robert Sobel, in his book *IBM: Colossus in Transition*, says, "War has been for IBM a significant catalyst for innovation." During the half-decade of World War II more crucial inventions were achieved — including antibiotics, radar, jet planes and nuclear bombs — during the whole of the previous century.

Since World War II, we're told, knowledge has doubled every ten years. But, as Walter Cronkite observed, it's often information without wisdom. It's head knowledge without that heart judgment that made our fathers great. *The Wall Street Journal* ponders whether "the American dream that technology can cure all ills will ultimately prove to be a Utopian solution or a Frankenstein monster."

Real knowledge begins when people come to know Jesus Christ as Savior. Paul's great aspiration was "that I may know him [Christ], and the power of his resurrection" (Phil. 3:10). This is the plumb line by which these inventions must be measured to determine whether or not they contribute in the final analysis to progress or impending disaster.

Evil Uncorked

The priest who served as Pope John Paul II's Japanese host during the pontiff's vist to Hiroshima bore scars from the heat and radiation of the nuclear incineration of 1945. Others in the crowd suffered from anemia, blood diseases and sterility inflicted by that holocaust. The pope commented, "Technological development for its own sake" is one of the tragedies of modern times.

The knowledge-seeker who opened this Pandora's box was Albert Einstein. As the centennial of his birth was celebrated, someone recalled asking him what weapons would be used for World War III. Einstein had said he wasn't sure, but he knew what weapons would be used for World War IV: "Rocks!"

Einstein had made other apt observations that were to prove ominously prophetic: that great spirits are too often dwarfed by small minds and that "the splitting of the atom has changed everything save our mode of thinking, and thus we drift towards unparalleled catastrophe."

Einstein's pupil and acknowledged father of the atomic bomb, Robert Oppenheimer, observed wryly, "The physicists have known sin, and this is a knowledge they cannot lose." His allusion to Adam and Eve's indulgence in the fruit of the tree of the knowledge of good and evil, which jeopardized their access to the tree of life, was apt. Man has come full circle.

The late Eric Hoffer, labor leader turned pundit, said: "A pregnant swollen world is writhing in labor, and everywhere untrained quacks are officiating as obstetricians. These quacks say that the only way the new era can be born is by Caesarean operation. They lust to rip the belly of the world open."

How close this resembles the warnings of the Bible. Paul, describing the "sudden destruction" that will come, said that humankind would be like a pregnant woman in painful travail (1 Thess. 5:3). Believers waiting for the delivery would rejoice when it did occur. Meanwhile, the world around would convulse in anguish.

A Tidal Wave of Change

Not only has most of this century produced dramatic advances in knowledge and technology, but "the next five to ten years will produce more dramatic changes than the last fifty," projects futurist Emil Gaverluk.

Alvin Toffler, author of *Future Shock*, reasons in *The Third Wave* that man is moving from the industrial society to the "electronic cottage family," in which in place of hand labor people stay at home with their computers and engage their mind power. "We are going from an energy system based on fossil fuels to one based on multiplicity.

Diversity will replace uniformity," predicted Toffler. He pointed to the highly industrialized cities of the northern United States, such as Detroit, that are in decline, while the specialized computer and communication industries of the Sunbelt flourish.

It was only twenty years ago that the revolutionary computer chips replaced bulky transistors. A *Newsweek* article explains how Bell Laboratories can place on a chip the size of a fingernail 262,000 separate items of information — four times the capacity of anything previously manufactured. A university library can be placed in one's shirt pocket.

The same kinds of quantum leaps have been made with computer speed. An MIT computer can perform one hundred billion transactions per second. By punching a few keys on a low-cost home computer, in a split second we can retrieve information from libraries, banks, stock exchanges and supermarkets. And as these data bank systems are refined, we'll be able to interact more and more, executing purchasing choices and other decisions with the flick of our fingers. Literally, we'll let our fingers do the walking rather than our cars being embroiled in traffic jams.

Certainly more workers in the 1990s are staying away from the assembly lines and making their living at the panel of a computer terminal. The American Association for the Advancement of Science projects that by the late 1990s 95 percent of those working will be involved in some phase of the "information society."

A Learning Explosion

Further evidence of this prophesied knowledge explosion is the fact that 70 percent of all the scientists of history are alive today. There are forty thousand scientific journals being published regularly, and a half-million new books annually. In a single generation Canada, a typical Western democracy, has increased its numbers of annual university graduates by 700 percent; India, a Third World country, by 1,000 percent.

In the field of medicine, Dr. Malcolm Todd, an American Medical Association president, reckons, "About half of medical knowledge is outdated every ten years." Seventy-five percent of the current medicines in use are ones which have been developed in this generation.

What makes the learning explosion even more revealing of end times is that biblical prophecy revolves around the Middle East, with primary attention to Israel. As we examine the growth of knowledge and technology, it should not surprise us to see Israel or Jewish people playing a disproportionately large role.

Although only one in 270 people throughout the world is Jewish, approximately one in three of the crucial inventions and improvisations in science and technology during this century has been made by Jews of various countries. It explains how modern Israelis living on such a tiny sliver of land can so rapidly assimilate the millions of returning Jews into such a thriving society. Any serious study of Bible prophecy needs to give special consideration to tiny Israel, where only one in one thousand of the world's population lives. The *Jewish Gazette* notes that "Israel's achievements in the technological field include the most sophisticated computer systems in the world...the most advanced vehicle performance tester" and "surgical lasers." Numerous other firsts and frontiers of research are named. Jews, of course, invented the engines of war, all the way from nuclear bombs to the sophisticated guidance systems in the vehicles that are able to deliver them.

The Robot Invasion

Automation continues to take over more and more tasks at the workbench, the switchboard, the assembly line and — in the future, we're told — in the household. Robots may even be able to perform intricate tasks such as cooking and cleaning. Robots are to the blue-collar worker what computers are to the white-collar worker. Even now there are seventy thousand such robots in Japanese factories.

Val Sears, reporting from the Washington Conference of the American Association for the Advancement of Science, wrote of how cyberneticists — robotic scientists — can already imitate the behavior of men. Robots can "exhibit curiosity, learn from their mistakes, be creative in the sense that they can look for purposes which they can fulfill, reproduce themselves, and have an unlimited life span through a capacity for self-repair."

"In short," says cyberneticist D. Rorvik, "a generation of robots is rapidly evolving, a breed that can see, read, talk, learn and even feel emotions."

The "groundwork has been laid," adds Lehman Wilzig, "for the arrival in the not-too-distant future of artificially intelligent machines — 'humanoids' — which will exhibit all the important qualities and traits characteristic of man." Isaac Asimov even predicts we'll have to institute legislation which he labels "laws of robotics."

Sears cautions that we have on our hands "the Frankenstein horror of a creature turning on its creator."

We're getting more and more to the place where we program men to act like machines and machines to act like men; to the place where we're humanizing machines and deifying humans. A recent prime minister of India regrets that the fine line between life and machine, between the animate and inanimate, is so thin that man is scarcely able to recognize where one ends and the other begins. It's the new pantheism.

The Seductive Screen

CNN's worldwide viewership during Desert Storm was close to three times the number of viewers during the period that followed. Even the intervening Super Bowl was dull in comparison. Billions of people could hardly wait for a newscast on the war's most intricate development. The technology involved was intoxicating.

The war was grimly factual. But the same mind-boggling technology is equally popular for fantasy-uses, particularly with youth. A *Time* magazine cover story detailed how the $5 billion a year video game business — mostly dependent on television screens for playing — has saturated America. Probably no other technological invention in a single generation has influenced modern society for better or for worse or has contained so much potential for the transmission of knowledge as television.

By the mid-1980s a ring of satellites orbiting the equator was beaming television shows directly from any part of the globe to every part of the world. A *USA TODAY* story on September 14, 1990, explained how CNN via satellite is watched around the clock in ninety countries around the world and that CNN had doubled its viewership worldwide over the previous year. A NASA scientist has described how future TV sets, the size of a large wristwatch and costing very little, will be worn by peoples around the world, bringing in programs directly from the orbiting satellites.

TV's Role in Armageddon

Television is more than an example of the proliferation

of information in these end times. It is an instrument of conditioning the masses for the impending Armageddon.

A comprehensive study of TV network programs indicates that violence on television is, tragically, still on the increase. TV depicts an average of eight violent acts per hour. Graduating high-schoolers have watched 19,000 hours of TV and have attended school 11,000 hours. They've witnessed via television 136,000 violent acts — 20,000 of which have been killings!

Add to this the fascination of wars dominating television newscasts year after year — in Vietnam, in Afghanistan, in the Iran-Iraq war, in Lebanon, in Kuwait. Even before Desert Storm scenes of warfare were where the most arresting action was. It was not just fun and games, like sporting events. It's the real thing!

Another relevance of television to Armageddon is that, as Billy Graham noted in a national magazine article, TV will be the means through which the Antichrist is seen and heard throughout the world. Revelation 11 prophesies that two witnesses in the middle of the great tribulation will be killed in the streets of Jerusalem where their Lord was crucified, and the people from the "nations shall see their dead bodies three days and an half, and shall not suffer their dead bodies to be put in graves" (Rev. 11:9). Merely a hundred years ago that would have sounded ludicrous, like some fantastic pipe dream or nightmare. But today TV makes such an event just another breaking scoop.

On a more positive note, there's the use of television in fulfilling the Great Commission. Jesus stated that preceding Armageddon, "This gospel of the kingdom shall be preached in all the world for a witness unto all nations; and then shall the end come" (Matt. 24:14).

Computers are now being programmed to translate from one language to another. A vice president of an

American TV network told me of computers that are on the verge of being so programmed that they'll be capable of instantaneously translating a speech into several languages.

This would be a step beyond what occurred in Hong Kong during November 1990 when Billy Graham was preaching. Watching him via television were as many as one hundred million people in many countries, each person hearing him in his own language through simultaneous translation. It reminded us of what happened in Acts 2 when the Holy Spirit sent gifts of tongues to the Pentecost gathering so that those from different nations could understand the gospel of Jesus Christ and be saved. What would eventually prevent the technique Billy Graham utilized from being expanded to all the languages of the world? The ominous side of this invention, of course, is that the Antichrist, too, could use this to his own ends.

Medical Advances

Finally, we read that in the "new heaven and a new earth...God shall wipe away all tears from their eyes; and there shall be no more death, neither sorrow, nor crying, neither shall there be any more pain" (Rev. 21:1,4). How our Lord will accomplish this we don't completely comprehend.

We often hear medical scientists say that man is going to live longer and that longevity has increased steadily over this century. Yet the increases have been minor. We still average little more than the proverbial "three-score years and ten." Although a few years ago a man lived to the "purported" age of 137, in 1990 the oldest person known to *The Guinness Book of Records* was 112 years old. Gerontologists tell us that it's simply not possible to push the average person's life expectancy beyond eighty-five. Death is programmed into the genes of human beings. Only God could unlock the code that presentences man to die. The second coming of Christ is the only possible way to supersede the laws of death.

But there is a clue as to what law God may utilize in His overruling death. It lies in research being done for the last few years by many thousands of neurobiologists, biophysicists, pharmacologists and other scientists. They are feverishly competing to find the key that will unlock the mystery of endorphins. Endorphins make up the brain's narcotic system, which controls pain, addiction, mental illness and — who knows? — perhaps aging itself. Says Montreal psychiatrist and endorphin researcher Dr. Heinz Lehmann, "We are discovering bits and pieces of a complex mechanism we knew nothing about until recently. Endorphins promise a panacea to man's ills." In that the Bible indicates there will be a millennium beyond Armageddon in which man will again live as many as one thousand years in his natural body, could such research lead to discoveries God will engage to restore longevity?

Man yearns not just to live one thousand years, but to know, as the rich young ruler revealed in his question to Jesus, "What shall I do to inherit eternal life?" Man longs to live forever! And Jesus has the only key to eternal life. He promises, "My sheep hear my voice, and I know them, and they follow me: and I give unto them eternal life; and they shall never perish" (John 10:27-28). Jesus is "the key of knowledge" (Luke 11:52). Indeed, He holds both the keys of eternal life and limitless knowledge in His hands.

SEVEN

"NEVER ABLE
TO GRASP
THE TRUTH"

ACCOMPLISHED DRAMATIST, critic, essayist —
such were the successes of George Bernard Shaw. A
Nobel prize winner for literature, Shaw worked his radical, often idealistic beliefs into his writings. Yet he saw
his intellectual castles come crashing to the ground, razed
by the specter of a post-World War II nuclear terror that
demolished his idealism.

Before his death he openly opined, "The philosophy
and the science to which I pinned my faith is bankrupt....
Its counsels, which should have established the millennium, led directly to the suicide of Europe.... In their
name, I helped to destroy the faith of millions of worship-
ers in the temples of a thousand creeds. And now they
look at me and witness the great tragedy of an atheist who
has lost his faith."

Shaw typifies many people in the twentieth century.
Though most people are not intellectuals, many are desperately searching for the truth but seem to keep missing
what is so obvious. They were described long ago by Paul
as "ever learning, and never able to come to the knowledge of the truth" (2 Tim. 3:7).

Does this have a bearing on the minds and moods of

the masses as man rounds the bend into the last lap leading to Armageddon? Jesus left no doubt that it does. There will be signs in the human psyche, such as terminal "dismay...and bewilderment" (Luke 21:25, Phillips). Paul wrote similarly to Timothy that he "must realise that in the last days the times" will be characterized by people who are "remorseless, scandal-mongers, uncontrolled and violent and haters of all that is good. They will be treacherous, reckless and arrogant, loving what gives them pleasure instead of loving God" (2 Tim. 3:1,3-4, Phillips).

This chapter will take a closer look at such things as stress, fear, drugs, meaninglessness, suicide and violence and how they take their toll on education, philosophy, media and the family. Their permeation of modern culture makes it apparent that Armageddon is not far away.

Rampant Emptiness

A surprise best-seller of recent years was *The Closing of the American Mind* by Professor Allan Bloom of the University of Chicago. Bloom's thesis was that "under the guise of open-mindedness, today's college students stand for nothing. They are 'nice' but nothing more." He contended that they are taught to shift morally and mentally into neutral, get high on hard rock or heavy metal, on booze, drugs or kinky sex, while slinking deftly around "values" and "ethical absolutes."

These students are not the first to feel this way. Some of Shaw's contemporaries — such as H.G. Wells, Bertrand Russell, the Huxleys and his earlier mentor, Charles Darwin — sighed lamentations similar to his, that he had helped destroy creeds but was left with nothing to believe in at the end. Their successors are such neo-intellectuals as Oxford's Professor Michael Howard, who, in *The Los Angeles Times*, observed that the whole climate of the thinking world today is obsessed with the possibility that mankind might one day feel compelled to initiate a nuclear war out of a lethal mixture of "hubris and despair." Howard continued, "Such a war might or might not achieve its object, but I doubt whether the survivors on either side would very greatly care."

Alvin Toffler, commenting in his *The Third Wave*, warned that as a world "we've hit a dangerous level of pessimism." A Gallup poll of people in twenty-nine countries confirms that the vast majority are looking, both in the political and economic arenas, to a bleak rather than a bright future. In Canada polls show that pessimism about our economic prospects outweighs optimism by more than ten to one.

If the public is so pessimistic about the future, how about the philosophic intellectuals? Christopher Lasch, author of *Narcissism in an Age of Diminishing Expectations*, saw man as "plagued by anxiety, depression, vague discontents, a sense of inner emptiness" and capable of achieving "neither individual self-aggrandizement nor spiritual transcendence."

Existentialist Jean-Paul Sartre died — his doctors said — because he didn't have the will to live! The titles of Sartre's writings — the most-read living philosopher until his death — often revealed his worldview: *Nausea, No Exit* and "Being and Nothingness." His message was that God is dead and so is man, in a spiritual sense. There was no escape from this dilemma.

Conditioning the Public

This empty philosophic posture fashionably espoused

by so many deans of academia has more to do with impending Armageddon than we might at first realize. David Manvel wrote to the editor of *Time*, praising Anthony Burgess's essay, "The Freedom We Have Lost." While calling the essay a "most articulate, lucid and compelling estimate of the failing art of democracy," Manvel saw a critical omission.

Manvel lamented the passage of a sense of individual responsibility for integrity that came from recognizing the source of integrity. "When this country was being settled, and later when it was founded, nearly everyone in it believed in God.... But once the psychologists and educators were able to convince enough people that God was passé, our democracy became a shell. Long after the life had withered, the shell survived. But now it has begun to crumble, and brilliant agnostic writers like Mr. Burgess are wondering why."

Someone else who read the handwriting on the wall regarding the secularization of society was editor Barbara Reynolds of *USA TODAY*, who in a March 16, 1990, editorial chastised the antichrist media secularists of North America. She noted how the press left out references to "Jesus," the "Christian spirit" and Czechoslavakia's role as the "spiritual crossroads of Europe" from excerpts of President Vaclav Havel's New Year's Day address. Even a news editor admits that the press is biased against Christianity, Reynolds wrote.

It is because of such anti-Christian secularism that Western man must be warned that, with democracy hanging in the balance throughout the world, we are being conditioned for a coming world dictator.

Abounding Iniquity

Psychiatrist Viktor Frankl, who popularized the phrase "meaningless existence," interprets the sex obsession of our times as modern man trying to fill a spiritual vacuum, which seems more and more to be a bottomless pit. Jesus warned of this period. He said that a sure sign of His imminent return was that "iniquity shall abound" (Matt. 24:12). A look at scattered areas of sexual morality shows that iniquity has found a fertile climate in the late twentieth century:

• 65 percent of seventeen-year-old girls and 70 percent of boys fornicate regularly.

• As much as 10 percent of the North American population is homosexual.

• The average homosexual male has 400 sex partners in a lifetime. As of September 1991, according to *USA TODAY* (September 26, 1991), in the United States alone, "The government counts 180,000 AIDS cases, 120,000 AIDS deaths. One million more are thought to be infected, many unknowingly. By 1993 the death toll is expected to reach 350,000." The cost? Seventeen billion dollars to American taxpayers.

• Syphilis increased 34 percent during the 1980s to its highest level in this half of the century.

• In parts of Africa 10 percent of the people have AIDS.

• Ten million children will be dead from AIDS as a result of their parents' prodigal life-styles.

Yet whole denominations, historically evangelical, are softening their stances on sexual sins. For example, Canada's largest non-Roman Catholic denomination, the United Church of Canada, decided in the late 1980s to ordain practicing homosexuals. The Presbyterian Church (USA) in 1991 considered a two-hundred-page report that endorses "the ordination of practicing homosexuals and the practice of sex outside marriage." It contended that "the moral norm for Christians ought not to be marriage but rather justice-love. Rather than inquiring whether sexual activity is premarital, marital or post-marital, we should be asking whether the relationship is responsible, the dynamics genuinely mutual and the loving full of joyful caring." Thank God it did not pass the denomination's general assembly vote. But increased permissiveness is a trend within Presbyterianism, within Methodism and within the Lutheran and Episcopal churches, as well as many others.

When Christian denominations have to struggle over whether biblical standards speak to modern immorality, we know that iniquity has gone too far. The end draws near.

Not just sexual morality, but values in general have changed. Daniel Yankelovich's *New Rules: Searching for Self-Fulfillment in a World Turned Upside Down* reckons that in the last twenty-five years some fundamental cultural views have changed in the United States. With the economy booming during the 1980s, many Americans were liberated from old anxieties about material success. The belief that hard work, self-denial and moral integrity were their own rewards gave way to the notion that the self and the realization of its full potential were life's all-important pursuits.

This phenomenon was characterized by writer Tom Wolfe as the "me" generation. But as Yankelovich assesses: "The people came to believe they could have it all — wealth without work, sexual freedom without marital problems, self-absorption without loss of community. Then came the shortages and the new austerity, and suddenly there was the effect on the corporate ego that a spoiled child experiences the first time he or she is critically denied."

One wonders, with all this dumping of pessimism on the public, how much people will really want to struggle to avoid Armageddon. Might man simply surrender, much as a hostage joins his captor, and inadvertently join the march to Armageddon?

Failing Hearts, Failing Bodies

Jesus predicted that with the mounting pressure of the end times, we'd see "men's hearts failing them for fear" (Luke 21:26). Why? Because they'd "realise what is threatening the world, for the very powers of heaven will be shaken" (Luke 21:26, Phillips). Consider the woman who wrote to Ann Landers about how to handle her "highly intellectual husband, who is chronically worried about nuclear war" and, overall, "extremely pessimistic about the future." Treating stress, often caused by fear of the future, costs $153 billion annually.

What has come to be known as burnout is one of the most common afflictions of many professions in modern times. Gail Smith, a corporate executive, observed, "There's enough pressure in a travel agent's job these days to pump up a truck tire." One-fourth of teachers in Britain, Sweden and North America suffer "battle fatigue" from stress in their jobs.

Professional athletes are breaking down under pressure. One national magazine contended that two-thirds of the National Basketball Association players occasionally or regularly take illegal drugs to "get up" for a game or "get down" afterward. One player said that as many as half of the National Football League players have used cocaine.

The stress is simply too great for many to handle. A former Toronto Maple Leaf hockey player was supposed to be a star in the National Hockey League. But he beat a retreat to Switzerland. "My life was a shambles," he told a Global Network TV reporter. "I'd go to the juice...had a lotta trouble with the bottle.... I couldn't deal with myself, let alone my family. [I was] in a void."

The same instabilities and roller-coaster emotional traumas are well-known in the entertainment field. Thirty-three-year-old John Belushi of "Saturday Night Live" put an end to it all with an overdose of combined cocaine and heroin, administered at his behest by his girlfriend for the night, Cathy Smith. Yoko Lennon recalled of her husband, John, that he had become "a recluse...he was depressed" — not for a day or two, but for years. In one of his most well-known songs, Lennon said he would give anything for just a little peace of mind.

The Ultimate Despair

Has all this had an effect on our young? *USA TODAY*, in the wake of the Gulf War, reported that "a third of U.S. teenagers say they have considered suicide. Fifteen percent have thought seriously about it, and 6 percent have actually tried, a Gallup Poll says. Suicides by fifteen- to nineteen-year-olds, which have tripled in the past thirty years, are the second-leading cause of death for that group."

The Chicago Tribune published a poll of teenagers that linked this phenomenon, at least in part, to impending war. It revealed, "Sixty-five percent of the kids thought a nuclear war would happen in the next ten years and that they could not survive it."

Others, such as critic Adrian Waller, point to rock musicians. The list of those who have killed themselves — whether intentionally or unintentionally, often with drugs or booze — is long: Janis Joplin, Jimi Hendrix, Jim Morrison, Sid Vicious and, in 1990, the drummer of the Grateful Dead. Other stars simply sing about death. Elton John sings about contemplating suicide; Elyse Wineberg says he is mortuary-bound; and British rock group Tin Lizzy belts out "Suicide."

Of the thousand a day who commit suicide worldwide, all too many are those who have climbed feverishly to the top of their status skyscrapers, only to find there's nothing there that satisfies. So they jump.

For example, twenty-nine-year-old Princess Maria de Bourbon, cousin of King Juan Carlos of Spain, was ravishingly beautiful. But she couldn't cope with the fatuous inanities in her circle of debutantes. She killed herself with an overdose of heroin.

This suicide epidemic is Armageddon in slow motion, in which the killer and the victim are the same person. The coming human annihilation will be self-destruction multiplied by 5.5 billion. But, thank God, Armageddon won't get that far, because Jesus Christ will intervene.

Increasing suicide in this age should not surprise us. With society dismissing the ancient norms of morality and family, there is little left for people to live by or to live for. Consider the disintegration of the family. Noted *The New York Times*, "With divorces now soaring to half as many as there are marriages, over a million children have their homes disrupted by divorce yearly. Under current conditions, one-third of the nation's children will go through this experience before they reach eighteen."

We saw earlier how fear of nuclear war has been suggested as one cause of teen suicide. That fear, often subconscious, is also considered a reason for permissive teen sex, according to Wisconsin sociology professor Ray

Short's testimony before a U.S. Senate committee. One only needs to observe the sexual breakdown in Northern Ireland over the last three decades to realize how closely a constant war consciousness and moral breakdown are intertwined. Life is so uncertain; teenagers wonder if they really have a future.

Escape From Violence

That constant awareness of violence numbs man's natural sense of shock and renders acceptable those things which we should reject. Take the matter of abortion, which is war to the death on the unborn. The most dangerous place to be in the world is in the womb of a woman who considers her baby not as a living being but as an "unwanted pregnancy." Sixty million unborn babies are murdered in the womb every year. It's all a philosophic softener for the barking dogs of war. It means that our hopes have to be fixed on God — the earthly dimension promises a sure holocaust!

War, of course, is violence and crime at the international level. Jesus assured us that as violence prevailed in Noah's day, so it would prevail just prior to His return. *Church Around the World* said in April 1990 that "violence in children's television programs increased 41 percent during the past ten years. Weekend daytime children's programs showed 18.6 violent acts per hour before 1980." It was up to 26.4 acts per hour in 1990.

In the spring of 1991 violent crime was up 17 percent in Britain, 10 percent in the United States and 7 percent in Canada. In Toronto murders in 1991 were up 80 percent over 1990. Senator Trent Lott reckons that "thirty-five million Americans are victimized by crime each year," according to the *Grenada News* (Mississippi) of May 9,

1990. At "this rate the Justice Department estimates that five out of six Americans will be the victims of crime during their lifetime."

Carl Sagan, writer of the bestseller *Cosmos* and host of the TV series "Cosmos Galactica," noted that on any given day "it's hardly out of the question that we might destroy ourselves tomorrow." He pondered, "Is there a cosmic Rosetta Stone? Can science bring us a message? Someday a message from distant space may arrive on our earth. The receipt of a message from a civilization in outer space would be one of the most significant events in human history."

Actually we do have the key to Sagan's Rosetta Stone of the universe. It's the Bible, a message indeed from outer space — from heaven! And more than a message, we have had the Messenger — the Messiah from heaven come to earth — Jesus Christ! He came to bring us life and love and hope.

As Bishop Handley Moule used to say, in almost every case where the word "hope" appears in the New Testament, there is a reference, explicit or implicit, to the Lord's return. Paul referred to it as the "blessed hope" (Titus 2:13); Peter, in his first epistle, as "a lively hope" (1 Pet. 1:3); John, as a purifying hope (1 John 3:3); and the author of Hebrews as "this hope we hold" (Heb. 6:19, Phillips). And, reciprocally, it's a hope that holds us up. As R.V.G. Tasker wrote in *The New Bible Dictionary*, "Hope is not a kite at the mercy of the changing winds, but 'an anchor of the soul, both sure and steadfast,' penetrating deep into the invisible and eternal world."

At age seventy Malcolm Forbes had climbed to the top of the intellectual, social and sporting totem pole. Just before his unexpected death in 1990 he was on "The Joan Rivers Show." Ms. Rivers asked him what he would choose if he could have anything he asked for. Without hesitation he said he would take eternal life. Within a few days he was dead, embarking on an eternal life that may have been quite unlike the kind he would have ordered.

Yet we can avoid any uncertainty about our destiny by turning to Christ, in whom we have "hope of eternal life...promised before the world began" (Titus 1:2). If you're in an intellectual state of "always learning, and yet never able to grasp the truth," trust Jesus Christ, who told us succinctly how we can forever become His: "I am...the truth...come to the Father...by me" (John 14:6).

Because we have this steadfast hope, we need not panic over the end times. Paul wrote, "Now we beseech you, brethren, by the coming of our Lord Jesus Christ...that ye be not soon shaken in mind" (2 Thess. 2:1-2). In other words, as Armageddon approaches, believers who focus their faith on Christ are to remain steady in mind and happy in heart.

EIGHT

A WHOLE LOT OF SHAKING GOING ON

ONE OF 1990's top news stories was the prediction by seismologist Iben Browning of a major earthquake on the New Madrid fault around December 3. People up and down this central United States fault line stocked up on food, water and flashlight batteries. They took mirrors off the walls.

Many top scientists dismissed the narrow time frame picked by Browning as nonsense. They were right.

Date-naming by seismologists for a specific earthquake is like Christian zealots picking dates for the second coming. Jesus said it's a no-no. But Jesus also encouraged us to be wise about signs of the times. He forecast that prior to His second coming, not only will there be "wars and commotions" (Luke 21:9) as we have examined, but also "great earthquakes shall be in divers places" (Luke 21:11). That is, earthquakes will occur throughout the world, and apparently they will be getting more and more destructive. When that begins to happen, Jesus said, "Look up, and lift up your heads; for your redemption draweth nigh" (Luke 21:28).

These proliferating earthquakes are to precede a mammoth quake that has been prophesied. Consequently, if we are really approaching Armageddon, we should be witnessing earthquake activity that exceeds any other period of history. Let's see more of what the Bible predicts and what has happened with earthquakes in this century.

Tribulation and the Big One

Coinciding with the increasing earthquakes, Jesus said, would be a time of great tribulation. There are several pertinent passages, but there is one accepted by Jew and Christian alike: "Watch, for the day of the Lord is coming soon! On that day the Lord will gather together the nations to fight Jerusalem; the city will be taken, the houses rifled, the loot divided, the women raped; half the population will be taken away as slaves, and half will be left in what remains of the city. Then the Lord will go out fully armed for war, to fight against those nations. That day his feet will stand upon the Mount of Olives, to the east of Jerusalem, and the Mount of Olives will split apart, making a very wide valley running from east to west, for half the mountain will move toward the north and half toward the south. You will escape through that valley, for it will reach across to the city gate. Yes, you will escape as your people did long centuries ago from the earthquake in the days of Uzziah, king of Judah, and the Lord my God shall come, and all his saints and angels with him...Life-giving waters will flow.... And the Lord shall be King over all the earth (Zech. 14:1-5,8-9, TLB).

The only additional clarification of this prophecy in the New Testament is that the Lord who comes at the nadir of the battle of Armageddon will be the Messiah, Jesus Christ. So we read in Revelation 16 that the rulers of the world were gathered for the great day of battle. "And they gathered...near a place called, in Hebrew, Armageddon.

And there was a great earthquake of a magnitude unprecedented in human history.... The great city...was split into
three sections, and cities around the world fell in heaps
of rubble.... And islands vanished, and mountains flat-
tened out (Rev. 16:16,18-20, TLB).

This Present Shaking

That kind of macrocosmic earthquake, as we noted, is
not due until it has been preceded by increasingly "great
earthquakes in divers places." That is what we're seeing
now.

During the eighties we read of an earthquake that jolted
residents of eastern Canada and rattled dishes as far south
as Connecticut. *The New York Times* reckoned that it was
the first significant earthquake in that triangular area
between Halifax, Montreal and New York since February
8, 1855. This earthquake was followed by three more
comparable ones and a host of aftershocks.

These occurrences have no special meaning on their
own, but they show an escalation of disturbances that fit
in with the emerging science of plate tectonics. Under this
theory, the crust of the earth consists of about a dozen
seventy-mile-thick rock plates that float on the earth's
semi-molten mantle. Where they meet, high-pressure
friction generates tremendous stress. Eventually they
break loose, and the rock fractures allow the plates to
resume their motion. That's what we experience as an
earthquake.

But an earthquake doesn't end with the shaking, according to such eminent seismologists as Don Anderson
of the California Institute of Technology and Don Leet of
the Massachusetts Institute of Technology. Once one
earthquake takes place in a region, it's like the breakup
of ice on the Great Lakes during the spring thaw. It's the

beginning of more to follow. *The New York Times* said that until thirty years ago not a solitary measurable earthquake had occurred in Colorado. Since then more than four thousand such earthquakes have been registered there.

Time magazine states that there have been more major earthquakes in the past twenty years than in the previous one hundred. In fact, *there have been more monstrous killers in the half-century since World War II than during the previous five centuries.* A network TV newsman observed that there have been twenty-eight macro-earthquakes since 1958, compared to twenty-four during the whole period before that since the birth of Christ. Seismology historians have calculated that major earthquakes have increased more than 2,000 percent since Columbus discovered the New World. What is more readily verifiable is that as many have died in earthquakes during the last twenty-five years as had perished in the previous two hundred years. Certainly many more people have been killed in this generation in earthquakes than in warfare.

There has been no shortage of devastating earthquakes in recent years. A killer earthquake struck in April 1991 in Peru, where an estimated 67,000 had perished two decades earlier in the most jolting of earthquakes ever to strike in modern times in South America. In 1990 there was yet another 8,000-killer earthquake in Iran. In 1989, for several days, the San Francisco Bay Area dominated the news with a blockbuster quake that struck during the first game of the World Series. The 1988 Armenian earthquake wiped out whole towns and cities, killing some 50,000 people. Two years earlier an earthquake in Colombia issued what *Time* called "one of the deadliest volcanic eruptions in all of recorded history; roughly equivalent to the A.D. 79 explosion of Mount Vesuvius, which destroyed the cities of Pompeii and Herculaneuma." The dead numbered 22,314. In 1985 a Mexico City earthquake took about 30,000 lives.

Earlier in the 1980s Iran was traumatized when 8,000 reportedly died in a major earthquake, an estimated 3,000 having been dealt death blows the previous June. Greece, that same autumn, was hit by an earthquake that caused $2 billion in damage. In 1980 Italy lost 3,000 lives — and Algeria 20,000 — to ravaging quakes. Back in the 1970s earthquakes killed 22,000 in Guatemala, 25,000 in Iran. According to the *Hong Kong View*, an earthquake in 1976 killed one million people and leveled Tangshan, China, where a sequel occurred in March 1991. The earlier catastrophe was perhaps history's most lethal natural disaster since Noah's flood.

The Hot Spots

In the United States, California's San Andreas fault has elicited for years predictions of an earthquake before the end of the century that could kill one million people and cause untold damage. This was the subject of a 1990 NBC production, "The Great Los Angeles Earthquake." Another 1990 network program focused on "Mexico: After the Earthquakes." It was a spectacular, if tragic, documentary on how awesome, as well as awful, an event a major earthquake can be.

Professor Raymond Arvidson of Washington University revealed that a fault line twice as long as San Andreas (1,650 miles long and as wide as 50 miles) runs diagonally across the United States from Washington state to the southern tip of the Appalachian Mountains in North Carolina. It was seen from space by a newly developed geo-scanner, and it could eventually be one of the world's most gaping continental rifts. This fault line could foreshadow a decimating macroquake.

But Bible prophecy was written from a Middle Eastern perspective, and that's where the highest per capita losses in earthquake disasters, with some exceptions, have been concentrated during the last few years: places such as Greece, Iran and Turkey, where, incidentally, all the churches of Revelation 2 and 3 were located. Judith Perera, political editor of the *Middle East Magazine*, writes, "So far this century, earthquakes have killed nearly 200,000 people in the Middle East and North Africa." The seismic belt reaches down from southern Europe and Southeast Asia through Israel and the Arab world into northern Africa. Since mid-century eight hundred villages have been obliterated.

The danger is escalating. "Only Israel has sufficiently sophisticated seismography to caution where to build and where not to build," contends Perera. For example, the Hilton Hotel chain wanted to build its premier showpiece to the world on the Mount of Olives. But the seismology engineers reported: Don't build! It's on a fault line.

That same location, as we've already noted from Zechariah 14, is precisely where the mountain will split to the north and south when the Messiah comes. The outcome is described in Ezekiel 47:1-12: A waterway resulting from the greatest earthquake in recorded history will open a river between the Mediterranean and the Dead Sea, which is fifteen hundred feet below sea level.

In the light of this, it was amazing that the Israeli Cabinet gave final approval to the digging of a fifty-mile canal to carry Mediterranean water across the occupied Gaza Strip to the Dead Sea, also for the purpose of providing Israel with 16 percent of its electrical power. Whether or not that canal reaches completion remains to be seen. What is sure, though, is that when Messiah comes to terminate Armageddon, destroy the Antichrist and set up His millennial kingdom, His advent will coincide with that behemoth earthquake. It will cause the river — the river of God — to flow from the Mediterranean through Jerusalem to a Dead Sea which will then be a sea of life.

A Tool of God

If there is any natural disaster that qualifies as an "act of God" — as insurance companies or governments throughout most of the Western world designate them — it's earthquakes. Isaiah 29:5b-6, for example, says, "It shall be at an instant suddenly. Thou shalt be visited of the Lord of hosts...with earthquake, and great noise."

On July 19, 1984, I was with Billy Graham in a crusade in Liverpool, England. This crusade was one of the most momentous movements of the Holy Spirit I've ever been a part of in my life. That morning I experienced along with the population of that area what *The London Times* labeled "the most powerful and widely felt earthquake in the British Isles for a century." The epicenter was within seven miles of the soccer stadium where the crusade was being held.

Nigel Hughes wrote in the *Liverpool Daily Post*, "I really thought someone had pressed the button." A local doctor recounted, "I'm a pretty hard nut to crack, but it frightened the hell out of me." (Would in Christ's name that it had!)

That night Billy Graham asked me to give a brief message prior to his. When he made the call for people to give their lives to Christ, over four thousand came forward.

No day in my life had ever so much resembled Paul and Silas's initial visit to Philippi. Certainly the earthquake that shook the Philippian jail where they were imprisoned did more to the jailer than merely awaken him physically. It awakened him spiritually with one of history's sharpest jolts, causing him to implore the apostles — in what author H.G. Wells labeled man's most basic question — "What must I do to be saved?" And they replied, "Believe on the Lord Jesus Christ, and thou shalt be saved" (Acts 16:30-31).

Fifteen years after an earthquake killed twenty-two thousand people in Guatemala, we are hearing that the number of evangelical Christians has doubled since the disaster. *Time* carried a three-page article on the miracle steps that brought "born-again General José Efrain Rios Montt" to power as Guatemala's prime minister. *Time* traced his remarkable conversion to Christ, his practice of fasting and prayer, and his becoming "an active member of the Christian Church of the Word, teaching Sunday school, preaching and serving as academic director of the school. So complete was his transformation that he often manned a broom and swept out the...revival tent in the church compound.... Rios Montt's rise to power was nothing less than a miracle." History will judge what kind of a head-of-state Rios Montt was. What's important is that the earthquake in Guatemala had the earmarks of being not only an "act of God" in terms of judgment, but it triggered a spiritual awakening in which tens of thousands turned to Christ.

Keep in mind that Jesus assures us, "Behold, I stand at the door, and knock: if any man hear my voice, and open the door, I will come in...and will sup with him, and he with me" (Rev. 3:20). No matter what "earthshaking" experiences we have in life, we can be sure they are sent or allowed by God to awaken us to the call of Christ.

NINE

"THERE SHALL BE FAMINES"

DESERT STORM was hardly a regional brushfire in terms of fatalities. Deaths may have numbered two hundred thousand, virtually all of them Iraqis and Kuwaitis. Yet, as high as that number is, only three months later about twice that many people perished when a cyclone swept Bangladesh. At the same time there was a spreading cholera epidemic in South America. And, of course, there was the high-profile tragedy — the flight of two and a half million starving Iraqi Kurds through frigid mountain passes into Turkey and Iran. It was reported that more were dying daily from starvation in that exodus than during the worst days of the Ethiopian famines.

Heading into the 1990s, the Soviet Union — with the agricultural land and climate to produce enough food to feed a billion people — could no longer find enough food to feed its own 290 million population. This was the most crucial factor in the revolutionary changes in that country, including the putsch that occurred in August 1991. It is well-known that whether the vast country turns to fascism, reverts to communism, or chooses democracy and free enterprise will be determined partially by whether the people have food or famine in their future.

Not just death, but *famine* was the common link among all these events. Like earthquakes, famines have always been with us and always will. But in that increasing famines, like increasing earthquakes, are prophesied to be a sign of approaching Armageddon, we should be aware of conditions around the globe. Famine is spreading on a scale that the Bible describes as an end-times sign.

Expecting Famine

Jesus' disciples asked Him what would be the prevailing conditions at the time of His coming again and the end of the world (Matt. 24:3). Jesus replied that there would be wars. In their wake there "shall be famines...these are the beginnings of sorrows" (Mark 13:8). Conditions worldwide will then rapidly deteriorate into "affliction, such as was not from the beginning of the creation which God created unto this time, neither shall be. And except that the Lord had shortened those days, no flesh should be saved" (Mark 13:19-20).

The United Nations, reporting on postwar conditions in Iraq, used the word "apocalyptic" to describe them. Indeed, what happened in Kuwait and Iraq shows how modern warfare results in hungry masses. The prevailing food crisis in the Soviet Union could cause the splintering nation to revert to war: internal and external. Hungry people will eventually incite war, and with modern weaponry being what it is, in its wake there will be unavoidable starvation. So the vicious cycle spreads from regions to the whole world. It's just another precursor to Armageddon.

Educator Robert Evans of France said that the world

is capable of growing enough food for the nutritional needs of its inhabitants, but that the main bottleneck is distribution. A case in point is the Soviet Union in the winter of 1990. After a bumper crop there were shortages of food verging on famine throughout the major cities. The result was that newscasts constantly reported omens of an impending revolution throughout the world's largest nation.

If for no other reason, famine crises will worsen because of problems of distribution. The aftermath of war dictates that the agriculture and transportation industries will break down. Situations become more and more complicated as whole nations scavenge for scraps of bread for their peoples.

This lines up with what the Bible tells us of the great tribulation, when Armageddon is beckoning. At that time none will be able to procure even a minimum of purchased food without the "mark of the beast" displaying on their hands or foreheads the number 666 (Rev. 13:16-18). The prophet Joel foresaw that when "the day of the Lord is at hand...the barns are broken down; for the corn is withered...the beasts groan! the herds of cattle are perplexed...the rivers of waters are dried up" (Joel 1:15-20).

We have this prophecy regarding the time prior to the return of Christ: "I beheld, and lo a black horse; and he that sat on him had a pair of balances in his hand. And I heard a voice in the midst of the four beasts say, A measure of wheat [which is about a quart] for a penny, [that is, for a day's wages]" (Rev. 6:5-6). Bible teachers are generally agreed that the black horse is famine. A look at Lamentations 4:8-9 or Jeremiah 4:28 demonstrates that black is indicative of famine scourging as a blighting plague, striding through the land. The imagery has even penetrated secular writing. *Newsweek*, reporting on critical hunger in sections of Polish society, referred to a "nation awash in black."

A Bleak Future

Earthscan, a British research agency, comparing famines in the late 1980s to those in the 1960s, concludes, "The number of people killed has increased sixfold." This is similar to the conclusions of the United Nations' Food and Agricultural Organization in Rome. It noted that entering the 1970s there were ten million people starving to death each year. By the 1990s that number had rocketed up to 62 million.

Pope John Paul II, addressing the Rome Conference, said poverty and lack of food "is the scandal of the modern world." The leader of the World Food Council sees conditions growing worse. "Food consumption will rise faster than output over the next decade, and the number of people starving will double to more than one billion." And when nuclear war strikes, as Desmond Ball stated to the International Institute of Strategic Studies in London, within weeks man can expect to lose one hundred million to starvation, apart from the incalculable others who will be killed.

World-renowned biologist Paul Erlich of Stanford University noted on "The Tonight Show" that there are whole areas of the globe where people alive today will die tomorrow from starvation. "There is not the slightest hope of escaping a disastrous time of famines," he said, for from this moment onward, "it is shockingly apparent that the battle to feed man will end in a rout."

Ross Howard's critique of the Worldwatch Institute's global report suggests that we "forget about using the word 'crisis' when talking about world production of food." Crisis "suggests a severe but temporary shortage.

The correct word now is 'climax,' meaning a final — and irreversible — shortage." Worldwatch president Lester Brown also lamented that he often feels "planet Earth is no longer a sustainable society."

With world population doubling twice in this century, the world's land is being worked so hard for food that one-quarter of the topsoil is turning sterile or eroding away. Thirty-four percent of U.S. cropland is losing its long-term productivity due to topsoil erosion. Iowa alone lost 260 million tons of topsoil last year (in a single year — something that could be said of Saskatchewan or Kansas). The Sahara Desert has moved sixty miles farther south into Africa in the last decade (150 miles since 1960). Florida, the source of half the world's grapefruit production and a quarter of all the oranges grown, will lose huge acreages of its prime citrus groves and farmland to drought, real estate development and other problems by the year 2000 if current trends continue.

The world's fishing ponds are in irreversible trouble. Brown insists they cannot produce any more than the maximum fifty million tons of fish they yielded annually back in the mid-1970s. In fact, they have since been tapering off. Over-fishing and pollution, concludes Brown, have transformed the Black and Azov seas from prosperous fishing grounds to dying waters in the last thirty years.

The Soviet Dilemma

When Ronald Reagan visited the republic of Russia in 1990, its president, Boris Yeltsin, presented the former U.S. president with an enlarged Soviet cartoon. It showed a nuclear missile on a cart, dragged by a tired horse, symbolic of the poverty caused in the Soviet Union by the arms buildup. If the manufacture of modern weaponry increases the already severe Soviet poverty, what would the engagement of some or all of those weapons do with regard to inducing famine? Such a condition is another harbinger of Armageddon.

David Dyker of the University of Sussex in England projects that the Soviets for a number of years have had "zero growth in farm output." An Associated Press article quotes a Kremlin report that, even prior to their present plight, in the last fifteen years the per capita annual meat and fat consumption for Russians has been reduced from 207 pounds to an estimated current 125 pounds. *The New York Times* reported that whereas in 1970 the Soviets imported four million metric tons of grain, that figure has escalated to forty-three million metric tons.

The Soviet Union, of course, has been undergoing shocking changes in its weather as well as in its politics and economy. It has suffered drought where it once had sufficient moisture, while in other areas there is unpredictable and uncontrollable flooding, which throws off crop-planning.

This, as journalist Val Sears points out, is not unique to the Soviet Union: "There is something awesome happening to the weather." The "CIA's World Weather Forecasts: Pictures of Major Disasters" informs us that "no nation anywhere in the world, especially Russia, China, India, and the United States, can afford to take lightly the ominous" warnings of the forecast for the entire planet. The report is truly a "chilling and scholarly" meteorological study, pointing to such radical changes in the climate as to cause its authors to warn that "the consequences in political and economic upheaval and international violence will be 'almost beyond human comprehension.' "

Delegates to the 1990 one-hundred-nation World Climate Conference in Geneva, according to UPI reports, were convinced "there is no doubt that we are fast moving towards the brink of a global ecological disaster [arising from the] global warming caused by air pollution and destruction of forests, [the chief offender being] carbon dioxide." In a 1990 International Conference on the Greenhouse Effect there was agreement that there have been foreboding changes occurring in weather patterns worldwide. Seventy-three nations, including the United States and Canada, concurred that global warming poses serious hazards to food production.

The American lower Midwest has experienced heat and drought waves resulting in losses running into the billions of dollars. England recently experienced its severest drought in modern times. In East Africa a United Nations official reported from Nairobi that from the Red Sea to South Africa's Natal province, it's "a disaster area. No matter what we do, millions will die." Gary Collins has said on "Hour Magazine" that this has penetrated Ethiopia and Somalia, where the deaths from starvation may yet run to several million.

An Overburdened Earth

In its January 2, 1989, issue, *Time* published a thirty-three-page cover story on man's contribution to impending famine. The article, "Endangered Earth," said, "This year the earth spoke, like God warning Noah of the deluge, and people began to listen." Writer Grant Jeffrey pointed out that in the book of Revelation God warns that the nations will be judged, that He will surely "destroy them which destroy the earth" (Rev. 11:18).

Time observes that the world's population in 1928 was one billion-plus, but in 1989 it had grown to five billion-plus and was projected to double again in forty more years. "The frightening irony is that this exponential growth in the human population — the very sign of Homo sapiens' success as an organism — could doom the earth as a human habitat." The reason given is not so much the sheer numbers, though forty thousand babies die of starvation each day in Third World countries, but the reckless way in which humanity has treated its planetary host. Like the evil genies that flew from Pandora's box, technological advances have provided the means of upsetting nature's equilibrium, that intricate set of biological, physical and chemical interactions that make up the web of life.

This occurs through massive pollution, the spoiling of resources such as lakes and the accelerating exhaustion of assets such as fossil fuels, forests and aquifers. *Time* remonstrates that universal man for many decades has been about as ready to hear of the perils of ecological rape as he is to listen to those "who insist that Armageddon is near."

Time stated that man's indifference to this life-threatening abuse of the earth is wrong. It highlighted how "pagan societies" taught that the earth was endowed with divinity, and mortals were subordinate to it. The Judeo-Christian tradition introduced a radically different concept. The earth was the creation of a monotheistic God who, after shaping it, ordered its inhabitants to "be fruitful, and multiply, and replenish the earth, and subdue it: and have dominion over the fish of the sea, and over the fowl of the air, and over every living thing that moveth upon the earth" (Gen. 1:28).

Time reckoned that never more than in the present has modern man been so awakened to the words of his Creator. Considering recent droughts, heat waves, sprawling forest fires, killer hurricanes and floods, and waste washing up on beaches, the magazine asked rhetorically if this was nature's "raw power" acting in retaliation to man's "insensitive exploitation."

Very likely so, in that "nature" is but one tool in God's hand. As the next chapter will show, not only natural forces but men bent on militaristic and other selfish goals are misdirecting God's resources away from basic food needs, thereby enhancing worldwide famine.

TEN

FEASTING
DURING FAMINE

DURING THE autumn of 1990 an estimated two million in the Sudan verged on starvation. A U.N. report said that in the spring of 1991 seventeen African nations were afflicted with serious famine. Five of the countries faced critical conditions verging on national crises. Widespread famine — not the superficial shortages experienced in the West — has been the legacy of such often-forgotten countries of the Third World.

The Minneapolis Star Tribune of September 16, 1990, noted that during a 1990 U.N. Conference on Development, held in Paris, the forty-one poorest nations in the world implored the United States and Japan to devote two tenths of a percent of their gross national products to public development aid. But the United States and Japan refused to set aside any portion of their gross national products to help the developing countries. Canada and the countries of Western Europe adopted the same posture.

The West does not have the will or the altruism that it once had to feed even a fraction of the world's hungry. This is particularly tragic because with modern advances in agriculture farm productivity has reached new heights. So much could be done to alleviate world hunger. Yet, as we will see, not only are there natural causes leading to increased famine, but as Scripture prophesied, there are hordes of leaders unwilling to do the obvious when it comes to trying to prevent famine.

Multiplying Mouths to Feed

Brutal hunger is most acute where the population explosion is sharpest in the Third World. With the human family adding 90 million people per year, for a projected world population of 6.35 billion by the end of the century, 90 percent of this increase will take place in the poorest countries of Asia, Africa and Latin America.

In seven of Europe's countries there are only five births per one thousand people annually — similar to North America — whereas India's rate is thirty-four and Ethiopia's forty-eight. American and Canadian mothers have about two children. In Kenya the average mother has about eight children; throughout black Africa the average is six.

One of the pathetic outcomes, of course, is child fatalities. Major Eva Den Hartog of the International Salvation Army lamented in the September 22, 1990, *Toronto Globe and Mail*, after returning from her Third World trek, "Fifty million children...die annually...from starvation." Millions more are casualties to "whooping cough, diphtheria, tuberculosis and polio, formerly nearly nonexistent in the Third World, [striking] 70 percent of children born this year [1990]."

Hearing of such poverty and tragedy, you feel ashamed that, according to a Gallup polling of Canadians, "only half as many of our people offer grace before their meals, as did so in 1962." This in itself is a fulfillment of Paul's forecast that "in the last days perilous times shall come. For men shall be...unthankful" (2 Tim. 3:1-2).

Inedible Guns

Look around the globe and you will find no shortage of "unthankful" leaders, eager to squander their blessed resources on instruments of war. It is a tragic irony, as *Time* noted, that amidst bountiful supplies of weaponry, leaders in Mozambique and Zimbabwe are saying both to the Soviets and to the Americans, "We can't eat guns." This is the never-ending tug-of-war between armaments and public welfare, particularly food.

The World Bank notes that "if a 10 percent reduction in military spending by the North Atlantic Treaty Organization were directed to the poor," it would double global aid. It also laments "the surge in military spending" by the poorest nations of the Third World, whose arms imports "average $22 billion (U.S.) annually." This turns too often on "the larcenous and tyrannous character of the elites of Third World countries," according to a report in the *Toronto Globe and Mail* of September 22, 1990.

As Lance Taylor points out in *The New York Times*, India, handicapped with the largest famine toll in the world, still manages to manufacture nuclear weapons. India did this initially from a Canadian Candu nuclear reactor, which was negotiated on the basis of its being strictly for the production of electricity. In addition, India is into a multibillion-dollar annual armaments buildup. Ethiopia is another desperately poor country heavily involved in a huge armaments procurement.

But do these nations only stockpile the weapons? No! They use them. *The New York Times* figures that since the Vietnam War, "countries in Indo-China, the Indian Subcontinent, Southwest Asia, the Horn of Africa, Southern Africa, West Africa and Central America all fought full-scale wars." The Middle East, where Armageddon will be fought, is perpetually at war or engaging in the hottest "rumours of wars" (Matt. 24:6).

President Eisenhower, who saw more of war than any of his predecessors or successors, rightly said, "Every gun that is built, every warship launched, is a theft from those who hunger and are not fed." Armaments world-wide jumped during the 1980s from an annual expendi-ture of $350 billion to $1 trillion a year. Most people would agree with Pierre Trudeau that "the prospect of a new arms race at a time when billions of people are dying of hunger is a veritable scandal. If we were to set aside for peaceful uses just two weeks' worth of global military spending, it could be used to turn life around for tens of millions of people." But it's not going to happen. For the two or three years prior to August 2, 1990, disarmament was in vogue. Then it was tragically silenced by Saddam Hussein. Diplomatic pragmatists, who insisted we keep our powder dry, were once again in the majority. The turning again of plowshares into swords was resumed in earnest.

A hungry man is going to fight for food. When the Australian prime minister hosted world leaders in dia-logue, a part of what has come to be known as the Melbourne Declaration alluded to "the protracted assault on human dignity; and the deprivation from which many millions in developing countries suffer must inevitably lead to political turmoil." Such turmoil would be used "to extend the realm of dictatorship in the world." In short: *Hunger will be one of the horses the Antichrist will harness to take over the world.*

A Burden for the Church

Evangelicals are to do their utmost to feed, medicate, house and clothe the poor of the world. Samaritan's Purse, Compassion International, World Vision, World

Concern, World Relief, Food for the Hungry and MAP International are some of the organizations that are doing this — but none of them with the announced intent of ushering in a social millennium.

It is incumbent upon every prophet of God to exhort affluent Christians to be much more giving and compassionate. Salvation Army ambassador Major Eva Den Hartog is right, in her crusades across North America and Western Europe, to exhort us to shed the fat of overindulgence. Sixty percent of us are overweight, she states. Americans weigh a billion pounds too much, and Canadians one hundred million. In North America we spend an annual $30 billion on diet formulas and $22 billion on cosmetics. Those expenditures alone would make the difference between life and death to millions of people around the world.

But when all is said and done, Jesus said plainly that there would be ever-worsening famines in diverse places. As statesman Robert McNamara says, the rich are getting richer and the poor, poorer. During the 1980s the number of millionaires in North America rose 10 percent per year. It's a clear sign of the end when feast and famine coexist so widely.

Jesus said that prior to His return men's hearts would fail them for fear of those things about to happen. *Time* envisages that as holocaust threatens through the horror of impending nuclear war, or from pandemic disease, we can expect to see people "prepare for anarchy by retreating to the hills with automatic weapons, radiation detectors and the 'Royal Canadian Air Force Exercise Plans for Physical Fitness'; a few have taken to storing freeze-dried survival foods in their garages for a well-fed Armageddon."

Holocaust Aftermath

What the world faces in the wake of an all-out nuclear war exceeds any catastrophe the world has ever known. Such a nightmare was described by the *Toronto Globe and Mail* in "Nuclear Holocaust" by Dr. Donald G. Bates, professor of the history of medicine at McGill University in Montreal. Bates reckoned, "The survivors will envy the dead.... 80 percent, to practically everybody" will be seriously affected by "the catastrophe.... The greatest damage of a nuclear war is not just death and material destruction...but the creation of chaos."

The chaos would be biological as well as social. The highest expression of organization in nature is the living cell. Its molecules are arranged with such exquisite precision that it can perform unbelievable chemical feats, including self-repair and handing on its know-how to daughter cells. But bombing this delicate machinery with radiation creates disorder for practically everybody. Exposed adults would suffer damage to their genes that would be passed on to offspring. The radiation would produce premature aging, and the deaths from leukemia would be pandemic.

Radiation also disrupts the body's defenses against infection. If this were "combined with social disintegration, the result would be devastating epidemics...plague." Though Bates makes no allusion to the Bible whatsoever, it could be imagined that he was writing a modern footnote to the book of Revelation, or to Luke 21, where our Lord assured us that when kingdom rises up against kingdom, there will be famines and epidemics feeding off each other.

Bates pointed out that "bacteria, viruses and insects are highly resistant to radiation. In an all-out nuclear war, a heavy dose of this primitive energy could tilt the favorable balance of nature from humans to bugs. If the meek don't inherit the earth, the cockroaches will."

Bates insists that "current scenarios of a nuclear war postulate the release of...dust thrown up by these outsized explosions which would remain in the stratosphere for long periods...dense enough to reduce the sun's light." Before the Lord returns the earth will be struck with "fire, and vapour of smoke: the sun shall be turned into darkness" (Acts 2:19-20). Bates says that the reduction in "the sun's light will tragically affect surface temperatures and all terrestrial life. Any significant cooling of the earth's surface from such a dust blanket would be catastrophic."

According to ABC-TV's "Nightline," the six hundred Kuwaiti oil wells set on fire by the Iraqis in early 1991 had by early March not only dramatically polluted the atmosphere but lowered the temperature in Kuwait City by fifteen degrees. If nonnuclear fires can have this effect, what would nuclear explosions produce? Carl Sagan predicts that nuclear holocaust will usher in a nuclear winter of apocalyptic proportions.

Bates explains further that "human rights and democratic freedoms...would be the first social institutions to go.... With no police, probably no military at home, governments at all levels decimated, who will preserve law and order?.... Martial law will be immediately declared and ruthlessly enforced." Economic ruin, as well, will be pervasive.

Whose New Order?

Bates comes close to reflecting what the Bible prophesies conditions will resemble during the great tribulation. With such a future facing mankind, the only rational thing to do for those who are not ready is to turn to Christ, who warned us not to let our hearts be troubled in the face of impending catastrophe. Amos 8:11 warns that the "days come, saith the Lord God, that I will send a famine in the land, not a famine of bread, nor a thirst for water, but of hearing the words of the Lord." Four chapters earlier Amos gave that exhortation which is as relevant today as it was for ancient Israel: "Prepare to meet thy God" (Amos 4:12).

In the Melbourne Declaration, after wrestling with solutions to poverty, wealthy nations resolved that there must emerge a "new international economic order." One of the cynics was New Zealand's then-Prime Minister Robert Muldock, who dismissed it as "a pious declaration composed principally of platitudes." On the other hand, President Bush hardly made a major speech in 1991 without allusion to his dream of a new world order. New-Agers, too, have their mystical dreams of a new world order, though Christ has no place in it. Will the ideal happen? Not by human achievement! And not in the current world order as we know it.

As Christians pray in obedience to the teaching of our Lord, "Thy kingdom come," the plea "Give us this day our daily bread" (Matt. 6:10-11) will be answered in fullness only when Jesus Christ returns at Armageddon to turn impending annihilation into His true new world order of peace and prosperity. Ravaging poverty will be replaced by prosperity and plenty, as unprecedented conflict is superseded with calm.

ELEVEN

"ANTICHRIST SHALL COME"

OXFORD SCHOLAR Alex de Jonge, in *The Life and Times of Grigori Rasputin,* characterized pre-revolutionary Russia as a society in which the whole country seemed possessed by demons and redeemers, and few could tell the difference. Such might be a description of how the whole world will look when the Antichrist seizes worldwide power — that is, a blurring between the sacred and the profane, the human and superhuman.

As C.S. Lewis used to say, it's a matter of realizing that the devil you can't see is worse than the devil you can see. It was with this thought in mind that Paul wrote, "Satan himself is transformed into an angel of light" (2 Cor. 11:14).

Much talk and scholarship in Christian circles, as well as much sensationalism in more than a few movies, has focused on the Antichrist. Yet there is a sure sign, also demonic and of the same nature, that is to precede his coming: *a proliferation of antichrists.* We'll see in this chapter how this spirit has invaded our age, as well as how it has manifested itself in many individuals you'll recognize.

Expecting Deception

Concerning the pre-Armageddon agenda, the first sign Jesus pointed to was, "Take heed that no man deceive you. For many shall come in my name, saying, I am Christ; and shall deceive many" (Matt. 24:4-5). He gave this sign previous to His allusion to "wars and rumours of wars," with the various others following these two. It was not until ten verses later that our Lord alluded to the actual Antichrist, identifying his advent as the "abomination of desolation" (Matt. 24:15).

But well in advance of the appearance of the Antichrist who precipitates Armageddon will be many masquerading messiahs. Each of these antichrists will soften the way for the revelation of the actual Antichrist, while hardening hearts to Jesus Christ.

Later in Matthew 24 Jesus prophesied that when seducing saviors and roving redeemers inflict themselves on the world scene, the craze will last more than one day. He made plain that during the great tribulation, as civilization plummets to its lowest point ever, there will be a degrading rash of Christ-pretenders. Deceived masses, grasping desperately, will be told, "Lo, here is Christ, or there; believe it not. For there shall arise false Christs, and false prophets, and shall shew great signs and wonders; insomuch that, if it were possible, they shall deceive the very elect. Behold, I have told you before. Wherefore if they shall say unto you, Behold, he is in the desert; go not forth: Behold, he is in the secret chambers; believe it not" (Matt. 24:23-26).

In the book of Revelation John characterized in considerable detail what the reign of the Antichrist would be like. But prior to that, in his three epistles, he made clear that while we are to keep in mind that "antichrist shall come" (1 John 2:18), we will be able to detect his imminent appearance by his precursors. John also indicated there will be "many antichrists; whereby we know that it is the last time" (1 John 2:18). Intertwined with these insidious "antichrists" will be the "spirit of antichrist" (1 John 4:3) and "a deceiver and an antichrist" (2 John 7). Such characterizations apply to much that passes for religion today.

Mini-antichrists

As the last decade of this millennium was about to begin, TV screens throughout most of the world flashed this headline: "WE BRING YOU TIDINGS OF GREAT JOY. THE ANTICHRIST HAS DIED ON CHRISTMAS DAY." Repeated from Romanian broadcasts, this was the announcement of the execution of communist dictators Nicolae and Elena Ceausescu by the Salvation Front. The couple had held the country in a grip of terror for years.

Another tyrant overthrown about that time was Manuel Noriega, Panama's self-confessed "maximum leader." The January 1, 1990, issue of *Time* noted that his houses were decorated with pictures of his hero, Adolf Hitler, along with profuse collections of pornography. And in one of his hideouts, beside the usual "fifty kilos of cocaine," was "a bucket of blood and entrails...used for occult rites." Like Ceausescu, Noriega also played the part of a latter-day antichrist.

The media is still discussing the late Bhagwan Shree Rajneesh, who took over a sixty-four-thousand-acre commune in Oregon during the 1980s. He sought to dominate a whole county on the south side of the Columbia River with his own people's votes. From that base he announced his plan to take over not only the county, but next the country, then the continent and eventually the world.

This man crowned himself the very "christ" [sic] to

thousands of followers who had come from all over North America to genuflect in adulation as he daily paraded by with his entourage in one of his seventy-eight Rolls Royces.

One of the commune's defectors told me that 80 percent of the commune members were college graduates. He estimated that 20 percent had earned doctorates and 12 percent double doctorates. An astonishing percentage had been members of churches or synagogues. These people were always learning but never able to grasp the one Truth, Jesus Christ!

Many were in a state of burnout before they had dropped out, tuned in and turned on to this masquerading messiah who assured them that when the coming holocaust struck the world, he would emerge into his rightful role as universal christ. But before the 1980s gave way to the nineties, the Bhagwan was ejected, returning to India. Soon he died, just another burnt-out guru.

Eager to Believe

But what has not died is the burgeoning "spirit of antichrist" (1 John 4:3). The Bible warns us "that in the latter times some shall depart from the faith, giving heed to seducing spirits, and doctrines of devils; speaking lies in hypocrisy; having their conscience seared with a hot iron" (1 Tim. 4:1-2).

The March 25, 1991, *U.S. News and World Report* included an article on "The Devil's Metamorphosis." It said that whereas "the Age of Reason undermined Satan's reputation...the wars and genocide of the twentieth century have brought his existence, power and savaging of society again to the fore."

A Captive Culture

We know that Satan has made his mark with youth. George Gallup's youth survey in March 1989 revealed that 95 percent of teenagers said they believed in at least one supernatural phenomenon, such as angels, astrology, extrasensory perception, witchcraft, Bigfoot, ghosts, clairvoyance or the Loch Ness monster. Belief in astrology is now 18 percent higher than it was ten years ago. Witchcraft believers are up 4 percent. Patricia Ryan, who has made an intensive study of the occult since her father, Congressman Leo Ryan, was slain by Jim Jones's followers ten years ago, claims ten million Americans are currently active in satanic cult worship.

While many people keep a distance from anything that smacks of cultishness, almost everybody watches movies. Hollywood has made it difficult for viewers to escape the supernatural and satanic realms by producing such films as the three *Exorcist* movies, *Ghost*, *The First Power*, *Devil in a Blue Dress*, *Dance With the Devil*, *Lucifer's Child*, *The Idolmaker*, *The Possessed* and *The Windwalker*, to mention but a smattering.

In the books of Daniel and Revelation the Antichrist is frequently referred to as "the beast." Certainly Hollywood is on to this with offerings such as *The Beast*, *The Little Beast* and other stories that deal with the Antichrist.

Most Christians would write off as harmless the movies and TV series that feature figures with superior strength or abilities from outer space. Yet these serve as conditioners, preparing the human psyche for the Antichrist, who will promise to solve the problems that have checkmated modern man as we wrestle with crime, disease, poverty, alienation and a feeling of being overwhelmed by forces far beyond our capacity to control.

This messiah-imaging is growing ever larger in sports.

When ace Canadian Grand Prix race driver Gilles Ville-neuve was killed, Maurice Moyrond wept publicly, "For me, he was a god." Confessed Gary Jones in *The Toronto Star*, "Hockey is my religion," with Wayne Gretzky his god.

What effect does all this have on the heroes them-selves? It's a yo-yo thing. At the top is self-deification. At the bottom is suicide. The decompression journey from fame to anonymity is one which many celebrated professional athletes are ill-equipped to handle, the dis-tance from being a "Who's Who" to a "Who's he?" being too great to negotiate.

One also recognizes Christ-posturing in the profes-sions. One of my closest friends says of his brother, a surgeon, "When he buttons on those white togs and strolls up and down those hospital corridors, he's like a god." It's ironic that esteemed physicians commit suicide from three to seven times as frequently, per capita, as the general public.

I asked Dr. Basil Jackson, a Milwaukee psychiatrist, who his most unlikely patients were. He replied that they're all too often clergymen! Their parishioners put them on a pedestal and treat them as mini-deities. It goes to their heads, as they're perceived as paragons of perfec-tion. Along comes some crisis — such as burnout or, all too frequently, sexual lapse — and the victim comes crashing down onto the psychiatrist's couch. Some of them are virtual basket cases.

No scene, of course, is so dominated by personalities ballooning into satanic messiahs as that of pop music. The rock group KISS — its initials reportedly standing for Knights In Satan's Service — is a prime example. "The Elder," the band's all-time top album, was "concerned with a group of god-like figures who've watched over the planet since its beginnings in primordial ooze." The

Elder, explained *The Los Angeles Times*, is "an orphan boy who, through a succession of events, comes to save the world."

The Beatles had John Lennon claiming that the group was more popular than Jesus. Their manager, Derek Taylor, said as they peaked in popularity, "They are completely antichrist. Sick people rushed up. It was as if some savior had arrived. The only thing left for the Beatles to do is to go on a healing tour."

Britain's successors to the Beatles were the punk rock groups. Most notorious was Sid Vicious, who killed his girlfriend and then himself. His theme song was "Anarchy in the U.K.," in which he boasted of being an "anarchist" and "antichrist."

To what extent are some of these rock groups, who are high on drugs and low on morality and social responsibility, Satan-inspired? That's an open-ended question. In a highly publicized court case of 1990 the heavy metal group Judas Priest was accused of popularizing satanic lyrics, the alleged consequence of which was the suicidal death of two devoted fans. The prosecution failed to convince the court that this was so, but the matter lingers heavily in the minds of many parents whose children listen to such music. Cardinal John O'Connor of New York made repeated appeals to heavy metal groups to remove their lyrics' allusions to the devil, but his appeals, for the most part, fell on deaf ears.

Many lead musicians are practicing satanists. The record jackets signal that we are dealing here with a sadistic sickness on the underbelly of pop culture. They feature satanic symbols such as children dressed like prostitutes, inverted crosses, desecrated churches, demons, skulls and mutilated bodies. These groups produce songs such as "The Antichrist," "Tormentor," "Hell Awaits," "Kill Again," "Praise of Death," "Necrophiliac," "Chalice of

Blood," "Forbidden Evil," "As Good as Dead," "Feel No Pain," "March Into Fire," "Show No Mercy" and "Evil Has No Boundaries."

When you reflect that these songs are jackhammered into the consciousness of the hearers by a belting beat usually played at high decibels, it's easy to see that heavy metal music is greasing the skids for a slide into the emerging Antichrist syndrome.

Pressured Leaders

Another reprehensible use of language involves words the media uses to describe politicians. *Time*, some years ago, could have chosen some better description for its Man of the Year, Lech Walesa, than to say he was a "Christ-like figure." Equally culpable was the reference to the late Anwar Sadat as a teacher and forgiver like "Christ." When the Antichrist does come, of course, he's going to simulate Christlikeness as a deception ploy. He'll be history's most monstrous deceiver.

John Fraser wrote in the *Toronto Globe and Mail* of a Canadian politician who realized his inability to rise to the expectations of his public. In retrospect, after a humiliating defeat, he agonized that the public places ridiculous faith in government to solve everything. The investment of such expectations not only devalues individual responsibility, but it also makes potential monsters out of good people. If we tended reality and our duty as citizens in a more intelligent and committed fashion, our politicians might be spared their current incarnations as latter-day messiahs.

This is such an intriguing phenomenon that some experts are coming out with in-depth studies on what it is that tends to make leaders megalomaniacs. Dr. Frank Elliott, a former British army neurologist, personally observed Stalin and Hitler and became convinced that the world's Neros and Napoleons have been made monsters by their crazed followers, who unwittingly exploited some strange weakness in these men. The victim lets the weakness grow into an uncontrollable malignancy until he ends up an incorrigible psychotic who loses his capacity for normal emotion. He will lie, steal, blame others — and all without the sensitivity to feel guilt or shame. Incidentally, all these traits were present in Saddam Hussein.

A Garden of Cults

Harvey Cox of Harvard University, in addressing a Harvard graduation class, suggested satirically that for any who may be unemployed, if he or she would simply announce his or her own divinity, the devotees would come crawling out of the woodwork. Billy Graham noted that there are at least five hundred such self-proclaimed messiahs in California alone. The late Bishop Fulton Sheen ventured that there was seldom a day in which a new Christ-pretender didn't surface somewhere in greater Los Angeles.

Father Timothy Foley, in his *The Cults: Signs of New Times*, explained that today more than ever "there is a spiritual void that needs filling." Apart from accepted Christian denominations and such other major faiths as Judaism, Islam and Buddhism, there are four thousand cults in North America. A shocking number have their own pseudo-messiah. Attaching themselves loosely or slavishly to these cults are some twenty-eight million North Americans. Moishe Rosen of Jews for Jesus describes how young Israelis are seeking spiritual meaning so conscientiously that they tend to become very religious Jews or they often delve into a cult. Few are as secular in their outlook as their parents have been.

Adherents of one popular cult, Scientology, converge in Portland, Oregon, to protest a $39 million fraud judgment against their founding guru, Ron Hubbard. Included in the marchers rallying around "Christ" character Hubbard were movie star John Travolta, jazz musician Chick Corea, folk singer Melanie and Frank Stallone (brother of Sylvester Stallone).

The Reverend Sun Myung Moon of Korea shows that messiah movements are escalating rather than passing. A Korean clergyman of sorts, Moon moved to the United States twenty years ago. Moon openly claims to be the "second messiah. Jesus failed in His mission because He was crucified instead of marrying and starting a perfected human lineage." Moon proposes to do what he alleges Jesus did not do — that is, as the new true christ himself, to keep up the momentum of propagation until his movement takes over the whole world. Those who visited the Soviet Union in 1991 or thereafter discovered that Moonies are spreading there like wildfire.

Moon actually says repeatedly on radio and television that he has just conversed with Buddha, Moses and Jesus Christ and that they have fanned his flame to take over the reins of the whole world, if not during his lifetime, then through his followers. He is off to a good start. *Time* reports that even back in the early 1980s there were three million Moonies in 120 countries.

Moon and his movement own and operate the *Washington Times* newspaper as well as many other interests in entertainment, fishing, food retailing and banking. Moon's dream is to wrap business, culture and religion into a global theocracy, with himself at the top.

The Escape Valve

The pervasive presence in our midst of antichrists and

Antichrist movements is a huge problem, but there is an answer. Jesus promised that "where two or three are gathered together in my name, there am I in the midst of them" (Matt. 18:20). Jesus, wherever His Word and invitation to "come unto me" (Matt. 11:28) are presented, receives people. Instead of brainwashing them as cults do, He heart-washes them. Instead of turning them into weirdos, He makes them workers, doers, real people — sons and daughters of God and heirs of His everlasting kingdom.

TWELVE

"ISRAEL SHALL BE SAVED"

WHEN THE dust of war had settled, Desert Storm had resolved nothing in the eyes of the Israelis or the Islamics. Postwar peace talks accomplished little. Billy Graham, who supported President Bush in his efforts to bring justice to the Middle East, said, "It seems that everything we do in the Middle East doesn't work out." In the final analysis the Middle East situation will not be resolved until Armageddon.

Jesus said that when Israel returns to her ancient homeland and is re-established as a nation, this will be the beginning of the final conflict. "Know that it is near, even at the doors" (Matt. 24:33). He spoke through the parable of the fig tree: "When his branch is yet tender, and putteth forth leaves, ye know that summer is nigh" (Matt. 24:32).

But Jesus' announcement in verse 34 is the one that carries with it such crucial import for our times: "This generation shall not pass, till all these things be fulfilled." The word "generation" is interpreted by some people to mean "nation." Jesus was saying that restored Israel — as a nation — shall not pass away until these prophecies have been accomplished. Link this to the psalmist's statement, "When the Lord shall build up Zion, he shall appear in his glory" and "This shall be written for the last generation" (Ps. 102:16,18, personal translation from the original languages).

Israel alone — its history, its modern renewal as a nation and many other facets — brims over with fulfillment of end-time prophecies. Many such events have transpired in our lifetimes. Many are going on now. Taken together, they give us a better view of God's history clock, which is ticking ever closer to midnight.

A Restored Israel

New Testament commentators are generally in agreement that Jesus' use of the fig tree refers to Israel as a people, a nation under God (Luke 13:1-10). Early in the crucifixion week Jesus and His disciples noted a solitary fig tree that was flush with leaves but barren of figs. Jesus, having the day before wept over Jerusalem for its rejection of His messiahship, and alerting the people that judgment was impending because of their spiritual barrenness, cursed the tree (Matt. 21:19), and it withered.

Jesus later used the tree in a parable: "Behold the fig tree, and all the trees; when they now shoot forth, ye see and know of your own selves that summer is now nigh at hand. So likewise ye, when ye see these things come to pass, know ye that the kingdom of God is nigh at hand" (Luke 21:29-31).

Jesus was saying that as the barren fig tree was a picture of Israel, about to be cut off, so the fig tree which shoots forth new leaves is a picture of a restored Israel in the era when "the times of the Gentiles be fulfilled" (v. 24).

The reference to "all the trees" could well refer to the

proliferation of new nations which sprang into existence in the wake of World War II, joining in the formation of the United Nations. These in turn are being joined by the many new nations of the 1990s, such as Estonia, Latvia and Lithuania. But amidst "all the trees" there was to be a special tree, Israel. So Jesus assured His disciples that before He came back to the earth amid the carnage of Armageddon, Israel would have returned to her homeland and become a nation again.

God's fulfillment of His promise to restore the Jews to their ancient homeland has its roots in His promise to Abraham four thousand years ago: "Now the Lord had said unto Abram, Get thee out of thy country, and from thy kindred, and from thy father's house, unto a land that I will shew thee: and I will make of thee a great nation, and I will bless thee...and I will bless them that bless thee" (Gen. 12:1-3). It is significant to notice that God specified the boundaries of the promised land (Gen. 15:18), and it included Lebanon. It's also important to note that God insisted the land would belong to Abraham's seed as "an everlasting possession" (Gen. 17:8).

Even when the majority of Jews rejected Jesus and crucified Him; even when the church was opened to the gentiles — this did not entail God's abandonment of the Jewish people as His chosen nation. Paul dealt with this theme in Romans 9-11. He asked, "Hath God cast away his people [Israel]? God forbid.... God hath not cast away his people which he foreknew" (Rom. 11:1-2).

Yet they would be set aside while Christ called out a people for His name — the church. Paul said "that blindness in part is happened to Israel, until the fulness of the Gentiles be come in. And so all Israel shall be saved: as it is written, There shall come out of Sion the Deliverer, and shall turn away ungodliness from Jacob: for this is my covenant unto them" (Rom. 11:25-27). This refers to the coming again of Christ as Israel's Messiah at the time of Armageddon. "A nation," prophesied Isaiah (66:8) shall "be born at once...as soon as Zion [travaileth]." As Israel corporately receives her Messiah, all her surviving people will experience spiritual rebirth.

So where is Israel's return to its ancient land prophesied in the Bible? The scriptures are so many that they could fill a small book. Isaiah 11:11-12 states, "It shall come to pass in that day, that the Lord shall set his hand again the second time to recover the remnant of his people." (The first time, of course, was when they were brought home from Babylonian captivity during the sixth century B.C.) And from where would the Lord bring Israel? From many lands, including "the islands of the sea" (Is. 11:11) and "the four corners of the earth" (Is. 11:12). Not until modern times could the Jewish people have been found in "the four corners of the earth," meaning all over the globe.

U.S. General S.L.A. Marshall was an astute observer of modern Israel from early in this century until the nation's repossession of Jerusalem in the 1967 war. He was convinced there was only one word to describe their restoration to their ancient homeland and their reoccupation of Jerusalem, against all human odds: miracle. The late Charles Malik, a Harvard University scholar and a Lebanese statesman who served as the first president of the United Nations, said that to ignore the prophetic word concerning the restoration of Israel to its homeland and instead to ascribe it to a mere humanistic "politico-economic struggle, is to have no sense whatsoever of the holy and ultimate in history."

A Tenacious People

This miraculous side to the restoration of Israel — indeed, to the very survival of the Jews as a distinct religious/ethnic people over the centuries — is even more remarkable when you consider the persecution they have endured.

When Jesus was on earth, Israel had been occupied for six centuries (from 586 B.C.). Our Lord predicted that within a generation of His crucifixion the land would be overrun by gentiles in an *en masse* massacre, and not one stone of the then-resplendent temple would remain upon another. In A.D. 68 20,000 Jews were killed by the Romans in Caesarea; and in A.D. 70 Jerusalem was conquered and the temple completely demolished. More than 100,000 bodies of Jews were thrown over the wall of the city, having for the most part been crucified, and another 100,000 Jews were sold at auction to slave traders from near and far. An estimated one million were murdered during this period.

Under Emperor Hadrian (A.D. 117-138) the Romans destroyed another 985 towns and killed 580,000 men (in what by then had been renamed Palestine). Jews were banished from Jerusalem, a policy which succeeding Roman emperors pursued relentlessly.

During the second to the sixth centuries Palestine was occupied, desolated and decimated by the Romans. Then for one thousand years the land was overrun by Islam. From the sixteenth century to 1917 it was in the hands of the Turks, at which time it became a British Mandate.

True evangelical Christians and Orthodox Jews throughout the centuries never doubted that Palestine would be reoccupied by a restored Israel. Both communities clung to such clear passages as Ezekiel 36:24, "For

I will take you from among the heathen, and gather you out of all countries, and will bring you into your own land." Prophesied Amos (9:14-15), "And I will bring again the captivity of my people of Israel, and they shall build the waste cities, and inhabit them...they shall also make gardens, and eat the fruit of them. And I will plant them upon their land, and they shall no more be pulled up out of their land which I have given them, saith the Lord thy God."

The promise of fruitful gardens brings to mind Jerusalem mayor Teddy Kollek's observations as to how modern Israel carved its fruit orchards and flower gardens out of a two-thousand-year-old wilderness. And even though the Jewish population has escalated to five million, 80 percent of their fruit is in excess of their domestic needs. Israel is only one of six countries that grows more food than its people consume and is therefore a net exporter of food.

In another amazing fulfillment to prophecy, Kollek noted, "Our second biggest export is roses." Isaiah prophesied, "The desert shall...blossom as the rose. It shall blossom abundantly" (Is. 35:1-2). Furthermore, the restoration would mean to "strengthen...weak hands, and confirm the feeble knees," and God's reward would be that "the parched ground shall become a pool, and the thirsty land springs of water" (Is. 35:3,7). This vividly expresses the impressive irrigation systems of modern Israel — implemented by faith and hard work.

Steps to a Miracle

How did all this come about in the twentieth century? A combination of Orthodox Jews and evangelical Christians believed in claiming the promises of God that Israel would become a restored nation, with Jerusalem as its capital. When these two communities combined in faith, God performed miracles — some of them judgments — without which modern Israel simply would not exist. British scholar Ian MacPherson points out that it was an evangelical Christian Jew, William Heckler, who wooed and won to Zionism professor Theodor Herzl, a Jew from Budapest, in the late nineteenth century. Herzl in turn won to Zionism scientist Chaim Weizmann, the first president of Israel, and Weizmann recruited David Ben-Gurion, the first prime minister of Israel.

Herzl, in 1897, masterminded the first Zionist Congress, held in Basel, Switzerland, where it was resolved "to create for the Jewish people a home in Palestine secured by public law." At this time there were only 50,000 Jews in Palestine among a total population of 625,000. By December 11, 1917, when British General Edmund Henry Allenby walked reverently into Jerusalem (he refused to ride, as Christ had done) and declared Palestine a British mandate, free from the Turks, there were 100,000 Jews, as compared to 700,000 non-Jews.

As a child Allenby had adopted the daily prayer, "Lord, forget not thine ancient people. Hasten the day when they shall be restored to thy favor and to their land." On the evening of December 10 Allenby felt a deep leading to pray and search the Scriptures — and he did so throughout the night. He was led to Isaiah 31:5, "As birds flying, so will the Lord of hosts defend Jerusalem; defending also he will deliver it; and passing over he will preserve it." So on the morning of December 11, moving his army in from Egypt, he issued strict orders to his British air force to fly low and in waves over Jerusalem — without firing a single shot — to invoke the Turks to surrender. The Turks retreated without any resistance.

Complementing this amazing conquest of Jerusalem by Allenby was the Zionist factor which, in cooperation with Bible-believing statesmen, produced the crucial Balfour Declaration of 1917 in Great Britain. It declared, "His Majesty's Government views with favour the establishment in Palestine of a national home for the Jewish people, and will use their best endeavours to facilitate the achievement of this object." The prime mover by then was an Orthodox Jew, Weizmann. He had succeeded Herzl as head of the Zionist movement and had worked for a dozen years to influence Lord Balfour, Lloyd George, Winston Churchill and, indirectly, even President Woodrow Wilson, all of whom were sympathetic, being familiar with the biblical promises relating to a restored Israel in their ancient homeland.

Joint efforts of evangelical Christians and Orthodox Jews have surfaced in other areas. The Oscar-winning film *Chariots of Fire* was such a project. Other Christian-Jewish film productions would include Billy Graham films *The Hiding Place* and *His Land.*

Also, as reported in *Time*, there is the annual International Christian Celebration during the Feast of Tabernacles (Succoth), which brings Christians and Jews together to Jerusalem. *Time* reported that these conferences represent "tens of millions of evangelicals around the world" who believe that the Messiah is coming to the world to install universal peace and prosperity, initially appearing at Jerusalem. These conferences draw up to three thousand delegates from some thirty-five countries. They include parades, cookouts and musical services.

A Painful Turning Point

One glaring episode in the Jews' modern history is the Holocaust. Did God have to permit this tragedy? Hebrew scholar Arthur W. Kac points out that previous to the Balfour Declaration in 1917 the vast majority of Jews lived in Europe and that this was still true up to World War II. Some had adopted a secular humanist outlook and were deeply attached to the countries of their adoption which had been their domicile for one thousand years or more.

Kac points out that the Holocaust and the establishment of the state of Israel in 1948, with the huge exodus of the surviving Jews from European and Arab nations, marked the end of the great dispersion — the longest era in Jewish history. History knows of no other instance of a people which, while separated from the country of its national origin for some nineteen centuries, not only retained its ethnic and theological identity but also, at the end of those two millennia, returned from far and near to its ancient homeland.

Kac, along with many others, insists that Ezekiel 20:32-37 encompasses the dispersion and the Holocaust that precipitated their return. In this passage God warns Israel that just when their dispersed people think they are a permanently settled and integrated part of the gentile community, saying, "We will be as the heathen," things would really begin to happen. It is then "saith the Lord God, surely with a mighty hand, and with a stretched out arm, and with fury poured out.... I will bring you out from the people, and will gather you out of the countries wherein ye are scattered, with a mighty hand, and with a stretched out arm, and with fury poured out. And I will bring you into the wilderness of the people...and I will cause you to pass under the rod, and I will bring you into the bond of the covenant."

That "bond of the convenant" took place when Jehovah covenanted with Abraham. It was affirmed in this century when Israel became a sovereign unoccupied nation for the first time in twenty-five hundred years.

Even then, but for the grace and sovereignty of God, the plan for the nation would have aborted. Britain turned the Palestine matter over to the newly formed United Nations. Turmoil ensued. On November 29, 1947, the General Assembly of the United Nations passed a resolution stating, "The Mandate for Palestine shall terminate...not later than August first, 1948. Independent Arab and Jewish States, and the specific international regime for the City of Jerusalem...shall come into existence."

But this almost didn't happen. A fierce war between the Arabs and the Jews broke out, in which the Israelis were outnumbered fifty-three to one and were underequipped. Nevertheless, they prevailed sufficiently to proclaim themselves a nation on May 14, 1948, with Chaim Weizmann as president and David Ben-Gurion as prime minister.

U.S. president Harry Truman recognized the new state, and the Soviet Union followed suit. Truman, in fact, was the strongest gentile supporter for Israeli statehood, according to Henry Kissinger and other observers.

Truman's efforts for the Jews may have helped him more than he would ever realize. Later in 1948 Truman had to campaign for a second term as president. In the greatest upset in American history, he was voted in ahead of a heavily favored Thomas Dewey. This was inarguably a vindication of God's ancient promise to Abraham, "I will make of thee a great nation" and "I will bless them that bless thee, and curse him that curseth thee" (Gen. 12:2-3).

On a broader scale, one of North America's keys to peace and prosperity has been God's favor resulting from magnanimous treatment of the Jewish people. Thomas Jefferson insisted that the new republic receive with open arms Jewish people into all walks of life to which they might aspire. Before his death Woodrow Wilson was a strong supporter of Israel's right to evolve into a sovereign nation. This has been true of all American presidents in the latter half of the twentieth century. It was Bush who in September 1991 placed before the United Nations the imperative that the 1975 resolution which had connected Zionism with racism be rescinded.

The restoration of Israeli statehood has indeed been a remarkable fulfillment of prophecy. We'll see in the next chapter that Israel's troubles, as well as its prophetic roles in end-times events, were only just beginning on May 14, 1948.

THIRTEEN

COUNTDOWN IN ISRAEL

MORE THAN half of U.S. foreign aid goes to a tiny country on the other side of the globe. Not some impoverished African land, not some Third World island nation gets watered by this stream of $20 million a day. No, this aid goes to Israel. In Israel's military alone, *U.S. News and World Report* reckons that Americans have invested $20 billion.

Why does this tiny sliver of real estate carry such clout with the United States? Why do its events make headlines so frequently? Why does it aggravate so many nations? As we will see, these seeming inconsistencies also line up with God's revealed plan for Israel and the role it plays in the end times.

Crowded, Hated, Scrutinized

Israel is extremely hard-pressed for space now that a million Jews from the Soviet Union are pouring in. This makes Israel that much more determined to continue settling the West Bank, much to the irritation of not only its enemies but even its friends, such as the United States. That is why in September 1991 Yitzhak Shamir finally avowed before the world that no one, but no one, would stop Israel from settling the "homecoming" Soviet Jews in the West Bank, which he refers to unabashedly as the "Greater Israel."

Of course, Israeli leadership knows how much it can get away with and still keep from alienating those who matter. As writer William F. Buckley pointed out, "It is unquestionably the case that Israel's political influence is out of proportion to Israel's strategic importance to the U.S." Pat Buchanan, the newspaper columnist who's regularly seen on CNN, greatly angered worldwide Jewry by saying there were only two groups that beat the war drums for Desert Storm: "the Israeli Defense Ministry and its amen corner in the United States."

It is said that Israel receives at least a hundred times as many headlines in North America as any other comparably populated country on earth. One possible reason is that the media of both the United States and Canada in particular, and much of the Western world in general, are masterminded by Jewish interests. It is estimated that 70 percent of the upper echelons of the media are Jews. The Jews coming out of the Soviet Union to Israel are, on average, in terms of education, a part of the upper 7 percent of the population. Gorbachev in October 1991 noted this and lamented the brain drain.

Jewish penetration of media, commerce and other strongholds worldwide is but one more infuriating aspect for those given to hating the Jews. According to the *New York Daily News*, "anti-Semitic vandalism, assaults and harassments increased sharply in the United States last year. The Anti-Defamation League of B'nai B'rith reports...anti-Semitic incidents were up 250 percent."

And here we see how this plays into Scripture. This itself is the beginning of the fulfillment of Jesus' prophecy that prior to His coming Jews would be "hated of all nations" (Matt. 24:9). The last vote on an Israeli issue in the U.N. General Assembly that I noted was 127-2 against Israel, something too typical to attract much notice.

Another crucial passage is Zechariah 12:3: "In that day will I make Jerusalem a burdensome stone for all people: all that burden themselves with it shall be cut in pieces, though all the people of the earth be gathered together against it." David Shipler writes in *The New York Times* of this burden: "Israelis increasingly are feeling the terrible 'burden of their modern nation.' "

Back to Zechariah: "I will make Jerusalem a cup of trembling unto all the people round about, when they shall be in the siege...against Jerusalem" (Zech. 12:2). Wrote James Reston of *The New York Times*, we have come today to look upon "Jerusalem, of all places, [as] not a symbol of spiritual reconciliation, but of division, hostility and potential war." So when we refer to Jerusalem, we're on the most volatile subject in both the Jewish and Arab worlds. We must keep in mind here that Jesus promised — in the times leading up to Armageddon — that Jerusalem would be compassed about with "armies," and that Jerusalem would be "trodden down of the Gentiles, until the times of the Gentiles be fulfilled" (Luke 21:24).

Jerusalem probably has not seen the last of outside armies. *World Press Digest* made the crucial point that "the Arab Muslim countries regard the Israeli occupation of Jerusalem and the West Bank...as a more heinous and long-standing aggression than the Soviet threats."

This is by no means to say that the Russians are to be shrugged off. It's well-known that the huge paw of the Russian Bear is hanging over the Middle East ready at any time to strike. But what will trigger their descent on Israel will be the Islamic factor: the "hooks" in the jaws of the Russians (Ezek. 38:3-4), spurred on constantly by the fact that entering the 1990s 37 percent of the Soviet army was already Muslim. The Muslims will never rest until the Soviets invade Israel. It is very significant indeed that the five former Soviet republics which refused to join their new "Union" of September 1991 are non-Muslim republics. Of the ten who joined in, six have majority Islamic populations. This is a crucial point to understanding what's currently happening in the Soviet Union. Throughout the history of the restored nation of Israel, every Israeli prime minister has reiterated that the real enemy they fear in the Middle East is the Soviet Union. The future will most certainly show that those fears have been warranted.

Is it any wonder that — in addition to the enormous weaponry Israel is "given" by the United States and others, including Western Europe — she is currently spending $6 billion annually on her military? At the age of eighteen, young men and women must enter the army for three years and thereafter serve every twelfth month. Virtually every Israeli over eighteen is a trained soldier. One in four of Israel's labor force works in defense-related jobs. This is the military effort Israel feels is necessary, claiming that the Arab states surrounding it actually have one million more men under arms than all the NATO countries combined.

Expecting Messiah

Will Israel's defenses be enough? Not on their own! A poll indicates that 40 percent of Israelis are fed up with the war syndrome and, were the right strong man to come along, would give him a close look.

"Democracy isn't perfect and dictatorship isn't all bad," said Yossi Sarid, member of the Knesset, adding, "They say dictatorship has its advantages. It solves economic problems. It weakens inflation, puts the trade unions in their place...why not try it?"

Concluded James Reston in a *New York Times* assessment of Israel's dilemma in the Middle East, "Perhaps then, if we listen attentively, we shall hear...the gentle stirring of life and hope. Some will say that this hope lies in a nation; others in a man."

A man? Exactly! Israel is yearning for the coming of the Messiah.

As Israel adjusted to its shock in the autumn of 1990 over Saddam Hussein's actions, the media carried articles on the hoped-for imminent arrival of the Messiah in Israel. For example, *The Grand Forks Herald* (North Dakota) of September 9, 1990, quoted fundamentalist Rabbi Mendel Fogelman, "What is going on in Iraq is definitely a sign of the imminent arrival of the Messiah. When? Maybe before you get this story written."

Of the seventeen million Jews worldwide, each who is true to his faith prays each morning, "I believe with complete faith in the coming of the Messiah; even though He tarry, yet I will wait for Him every coming day."

Israel's primary worry as a nation is security. This will be the open door for the Antichrist when he signs a peace pact with Israel immediately after the rapture of the church. Israelis' euphoria will be enormous. But they'll be betrayed. Seven years later the real Redeemer will come to Zion to introduce a worldwide kingdom of peace and prosperity. Jerusalem will be the capital, and Jesus Christ the King will reign from His throne in Jerusalem for one thousand years.

But there remain certain key events, with specific locales in Israel, that must first take place.

Raised From the Dead

A century ago the Hebrew language was as dead as Moses. Then Eliezer Ben Yehuda took on the impossible: to revive the language from the grave and to convince an entire group of people to learn it and use it as their native tongue.

To this cause he became a fanatic. He succeeded. Today Orthodox Jews are more strict about Hebrew in Israel than any Francophile ever has been about French in Quebec.

Such is clearly a fulfillment of the Zephaniah 3:9 prophecy: "For then will I turn to the people a pure language, that they may all call upon the name of the Lord, to serve him with one consent." And with the Hebrew Old Testament an intellectual focal point of Israelis today, the world is reading again and again of their dreams and visions of the coming Messiah.

Yet there is a second, and much more complicated, indicator of end times that involves Hebrew culture. In fact, Armageddon will pivot on this one issue: the Temple Mount.

Temple Troubles

When Jesus prophesied, "Ye therefore shall see the abomination of desolation, spoken of by Daniel the prophet, stand in the holy place (whoso readeth, let him understand:)" (Matt. 24:15), He was speaking of a temple in Jerusalem during the great tribulation. Paul elaborated that the Antichrist would surely come, "that man of sin [shall] be revealed, the son of perdition; who opposeth and exalteth himself above all that is called God, or that is worshipped; so that he as God sitteth in the temple of God, shewing himself that he is God" (2 Thess. 2:3-4).

Christianity Today quoted Sheik Saa al-Dinal-Alami, Islam's Supreme Muslim Council head, as saying that Muslims are prepared to die to keep Jews from praying on the Temple Mount. Meanwhile, a group of prominent Orthodox rabbis have issued a call for the construction of a temple on the Temple Mount.

Will the millennial temple be built before, during or after the great tribulation? That is a moot question. There certainly will be a temple in use during the tribulation, and certainly Christ will have the most glorious temple of all during His millennial reign.

In the 1980s the Israeli prime minister dedicated what Reuters news agency called "the world's most beautiful synagogue, a soaring $14.5 million building in the heart of Jerusalem. The Jerusalem Grand Synagogue...took ten years to build.... Some 1,700 oak seats encircle the marble ceremonial area." Many Orthodox Jews, as well as studious evangelicals, avow this will be Israel's temple of the tribulation. However, it will not qualify as the millennial temple.

On the other hand, there are those who believe the tribulation-era temple must be exactly in the place where currently the most sensitive building on earth stands — the Dome of the Rock. The Mosque of Omar (another name for the Dome of the Rock) was built first in the seventh century around the protrusion of bedrock where the prophet Mohammed, according to Muslim tradition, ascended to heaven on his horse. It is Islam's third holiest shrine.

One Easter Sunday in the early 1980s Alan Harry Goodman, age thirty-seven, an American-born Israeli soldier with an automatic rifle, shot his way into the Dome of the Rock, killing two and wounding nine. In Goodman's possession was literature from the Kach movement of extremely Orthodox Jews, led by the late ultra-nationalist Rabbi Meir Kahane. A *New York Times* article noted that this movement contended uncompromisingly that Bible prophecy promises that the adjacent mosques of Omar and Al Aksa must be replaced with a new temple because this is "the site of the original Jewish temple built by Solomon, and of the second temple which was destroyed by the Romans in A.D. 70."

In the mid-eighties twenty men were accused of illegal possession of huge arms caches with the intention of blowing up the Dome of the Rock Mosque in Jerusalem. They believed, according to their interpretation of Scripture, that the mosque is an abomination and that its destruction would prepare the way for the Messiah.

In October 1990 there was the slaughter on the Temple Mount of twenty-one Palestinians by the Israeli police. The incident was triggered by a group of zealous Zionists endeavoring to lay a cornerstone for the third temple.

Messianic Jews in the Last Days

When the church has been raptured to heaven, there will be 144,000 Jewish evangelists during the great tribulation, going forth preaching the gospel to the whole world amidst horrific holocaust and persecution (Rev. 7:4). It will be they in particular who will be "hated of all men" for Jesus' name's sake (Luke 21:17).

Billy Graham's longtime associate, Roy Gustafson, who has been to Israel more than 130 times, notes that the million Jews returning to Israel from the Soviet Union during the 1990s have among them an astonishingly high percentage of born-again Christians. Many are outspoken in their testimony that Jesus is their Messiah and personal Savior.

Sid Roth, a Hebrew Christian with a worldwide radio ministry, has computed that for the first time in nineteen hundred years of church history there is a larger percentage of Jews per capita being born again in today's world than gentiles. So joyfully he reaffirms Paul, "I am not ashamed of the gospel...for it is the power of God unto salvation to every one that believeth; to the Jew first, and also to the Greek" (Rom. 1:16).

We should expect that Jews in unprecedented numbers will continue to become Christians. Many will become martyrs, while other millions will make their way toward Jerusalem to await what the subsequent chapters of this book will explain in more detail — the coming Man on the white horse prophesied in Revelation 19.

FOURTEEN

"GOG, THE LAND OF MAGOG"

JESUS FORETOLD that when we "see Jerusalem compassed with armies, then know [that the end] is nigh" (Luke 21:20). One doesn't have to look hard to see an array of armies, mobilized in the Middle East for the most part, for the sole purpose of driving Israel from the face of the earth. In addition to Israel's own strong and well-equipped army, there are the armies of forty Islamic countries.

We are referring not only to Arabs. Arabs make up only 15 percent of the world's one billion Muslims. Muslims may have internecine battles among themselves such as the Iran-Iraq war, the Jordan-Syria skirmishes or the Libya-Egypt fusillades. But the Islamic military, wherever they reside, are agreed on one obsession: *the driving of the Jews from Israel.*

That is scary enough; but what is even more frightening, and particularly significant from a biblical standpoint, is the prophesied power to the north — Russia. With the Soviet Union having formed alliances with some of the key Arab states, we are seeing the chessboard configuration reach a very touchy arrangement that conforms with what the Bible tells us to expect.

The Soviet Menace

The Soviet Union has assembled the most potent military force in history. Noted Paul Robinson as he served as U.S. ambassador to Canada, the Soviet edge over the West is "two times in tactical air, three times in submarines, four times in artillery and five times in tanks." Experts in both Europe and America, according to *The Los Angeles Times*, reckon the Soviet army has a 2:1 advantage over the West.

Of course, there has been a great deal of upheaval in recent years in the Soviet Union, but *Time* cautions that the nation is quite willing to crank out weapons "while coming up short on light bulbs." An estimated 50 percent of its gross national product goes for defense spending.

How are the Russians relevant to Israel, where Armageddon will be fought? Jesus said a sure sign of His return would be hatred of the Jews, and nowhere has this animosity been more an obsession than in the Soviet Union.

Stalin exterminated six million Jews. In more recent years, noted the late Andrei Sakharov, father of the Russian hydrogen bomb, "The Soviet Union has raised anti-Semitism to the level of religion in a godless society." Stephen Handleman writes in *The Toronto Star* of a Russian Jewess belonging to the intelligentsia who left Russia for Israel in 1990. "It's not because there is no meat or sugar...or because my family lives in cramped and uncomfortable conditions. All that is true. But the fact is, I am being chased out, like a dog kicked outdoors. [It's because] we are Jews."

As for the intentions of the Soviets in the Middle East, Arnold Handleman points out in the *Toronto Globe and Mail*, "Russia [today] in the Mideast is as innocent as a fox in a henhouse." When Edward Shevardnadze submitted his resignation on December 20, 1990, he made it very clear that his backing the U.N. resolution to force Saddam Hussein out of Kuwait was being resisted by rivals who favored keeping Iraq as a client state.

In other words, the Soviets were showing every evidence of siding in the future, as in the past, with the Arabs over the Israelis.

Russia in Scripture

Russia is no shadow figure in terms of Scripture. Ezekiel 37-39 gives an account which evangelicals and also Orthodox Jews believe applies to the Soviets. Rabbinic literature dealing with this is both massive and definitive and is an integral basis for current Israeli government policy.

These chapters also comprise the most familiar and dramatic exposition relating to the return of Israel to its homeland, culminating in verses 21 and 22 of chapter 37: "Behold, I will take the children of Israel from among the heathen, whither they be gone, and will gather them on every side, and bring them into their own land: and I will make them one nation in the land."

In chapter 38 we read that in the latter days it will be asked, "Art thou he of whom I have spoken in old time by my servants the prophets of Israel?" (Ezek. 38:17). And chapter 39 makes plain the purpose of what we are about to explore: "Thus saith the Lord God.... So will I make my holy name known in the midst of my people Israel; and I will not let them pollute my holy name any more: and the heathen shall know that I am the Lord, the Holy One in Israel. Behold, it is come, and it is done, saith the Lord God; this is the day whereof I have spoken" (Ezek. 39:1,7-8).

What is "come"? What is "done"? What "day" is this? Ezekiel 38:1-2 recounts, "The word of the Lord came unto me, saying, Son of man, set thy face against Gog, the land of Magog, the chief prince of Meshech and Tubal, and prophesy against him, and say, Thus saith the Lord God: Behold, I am against thee, O Gog, the chief prince of Meshech and Tubal."

Jewish and Christian scholars have demonstrated that Gog and Magog (first referred to in Genesis 10:2) here refer to Russia and that Meshech refers to its capital, Moscow. In addition to the historical and linguistic clues, we note that they come from out of the "north parts" (more accurately translated: "very far north parts") (Ezek. 38:15; 39:2). The Soviet Union, of course, is precisely north of Israel, from which this prophecy was written.

Ezekiel goes on to point out that the Russian forces are supplemented by "a great company" (38:4) and by "all thy bands" (39:4), which could be interpreted as satellite nations. And as we've noted earlier, Russia fills the bill for having "all sorts of armour" (38:4).

Other Nations

Ezekiel 38:6 refers to "Gomer" coming with this Russian-led coalition against Israel. Orthodox Jews have no doubt but that this refers to Germany; in the Talmud Gomer is spoken of as "Germani." *The Washington Post* of September 14, 1990, reported "Germany and the Soviet Union (locked themselves into) a twenty-year friendship treaty, a document that is designed to create the basis for a new political and economic relationship between the nations after decades of post-war animosity." Stalin, like Hitler, killed at least six million Jews. God, because of His biblical promises to Israel, has accounts yet to settle with those two nations.

Ethiopia is one of the nations joining the Soviets in

their march on Israel (Ezek. 38:5). In 1974 emperor Haile Selassie, a Christian whose name meant "Lion of the tribe of Judah," was overthrown by hard-line communist Mengistu Haile Mariam, who, armed by the Soviets, perpetuated a Marxist regime there until 1991. Former Ethiopian journalist Dereje Denessa wrote in the *New Republic* that Mariam "propped up by Soviet forces has unleashed a reign of terror that has taken the lives of over 500,000 Ethiopians." Mariam was overthrown by forces who prided themselves in being "Maoists." With the Falasha Jews virtually all airlifted back to Israel, there remains a residual hostility to the state of Israel in the official ranks of the new Ethiopian regime. Ethiopia has the largest army in Africa; together with such militant Muslim regimes as exist in the adjacent Sudan and other north African countries, they could launch a powerful attack against Israel.

Iraq and Iran — biblical Persia — also are named with Ethiopia and Libya in Ezekiel 38:5. The shiftiness of Gorbachev in refusing to alienate Iraq was never more evident than in Desert Storm. While nominally supporting the U.N. resolution to blockade Hussein in order to retain their economic bolstering from the United States and Western Europe, the Soviets kept their five thousand technicians in Iraq, helping Hussein keep his war machines operational. As for Iraq, as late as autumn 1991 it was obvious Desert Storm did nothing to deter the determination of Saddam Hussein. As *USA TODAY* of September 26, 1991, stated in a front-page article, he seems committed to keeping Iraq on "the brink of a new war." He was continuing to defy the United Nations weapons inspection team, determined as he is "to hide...how close Iraq [is] to building a nuclear weapon." What for? To blow up Israel!

The other part of Persia referred to in Ezekiel 38:5 is

Iran. Henry Kissinger wrote in the January 28, 1991, *Newsweek* that the world can expect Iran and Iraq to come closer and closer together, perhaps by military conquest. And *Time* reports that a secret cooperation pact has been signed between Iran and Russia, whereby the Soviets would supply Iran with intelligence and security forces to bolster the Islamic Guard. Iran, as *Time* notes, "has signed several economic agreements with the Soviet Union." A Reuters report notes that as millions of orchestrated Iranians hit the streets to celebrate the anniversary of their revolution, they chanted, "Death [to] Israel."

The third country named in Ezekiel 38:5 is Libya. A *Newsweek* cover story refers to its strongman, Colonel Mu'ammar Qaddafi, as "the most dangerous man in the world," while *Time* judged him "the world's most notorious supporter of international terrorism." His intentions have not changed over the last fifteen years.

What is Qaddafi's foulest obsession? When he proposed merging with Syria, he pledged, "I will declare myself, Mu'ammar Qaddafi, a member of the fedayeen and will go join them to fight Israel. I am going to fight and die in Galilee!" It is significant that Qaddafi says Galilee, not Judea, where Jerusalem is located. For if Qaddafi joins with the Soviets in a war to obliterate Israel, it would indeed be where the mountains of northern Galilee rise to merge with the Golan Heights and the Lebanon Mountains — the same terrain where the final holocaust is to take place.

Bloodied Mountains

Expect the Soviets and their satellites, including Germany, Libya, Ethiopia, Iran and Iraq, to make the most horrible rampage of human military history. Their combined blitzkrieg will be on Israel, with the avowed intent to obliterate her from the face of the earth once and for all.

Orthodox Jews link passages from Isaiah 13,17,18,19 and 24; Joel 1-2; Ezekiel 25; and Daniel 11:40-44 to this terrible "battle of Gog and Magog," as they call it. Evangelical scholars believe they can see it prophesied also in Revelation 6 and 8.

During the 1980s United Press International disseminated a story about the dreams — reported to have been on the same night — of three distinguished Jewish rabbis that the Gog-Magog war was not far away. It was noted, "The chief rabbi of the Wailing Wall in Jerusalem's old city is sure Israel will confront the Soviet Union in a battle over the holy city. 'And it will be a nuclear war,' they contended, drawing in both superpowers."

Under what circumstances will the Russians instigate a nuclear war? Ezekiel 38:10-12 explains: "At the same time shall things come into thy mind, and thou shalt think an evil thought: and thou shalt say, I will go up to the land of unwalled villages; I will go to them that are at rest, that dwell safely, all of them dwelling without walls, and having neither bars nor gates, to take a spoil, and to take a prey; to turn thine hand upon the desolate places that are now inhabited, and upon the people that are gathered out of the nations, which have gotten cattle and goods, that dwell in the midst of the land."

Israel is exceedingly rich in "spoil" (natural resources) in a hungry world. There's enough potash in the Dead Sea bottom to fertilize the agricultural lands of the Soviet Union — where crop failures are legendary — for a thousand years. Other reports indicate deep reserves of untapped oil in Israel. Jewish ownership of "goods" and businesses worldwide is legendary.

Furthermore, "in the latter years thou shalt come into the land that is brought back from the sword, and is gathered out of many people, against the mountains of Israel, which have been always waste: but it is brought forth out of the nations" (Ezek. 38:8).

The mountains of Israel! Is there any real significance to Israel's annexation of the Golan Heights? Roy Gustafson of our Billy Graham team told me of an Orthodox Jew, gesturing toward those Golan Heights, who exclaimed to him soberly, "On those mountains will lie, one day, the corpses of the Russian armies, thrown back in their attack on our land."

I believe that Lebanon will be a massive crematorium during the great tribulation and a restored paradise during the millennium. What makes Lebanon so significant is that it is a country of north/south mountains in two ranges with two valleys between, connecting western Syria and modern Israel. It is the logical path for a Russian-led attack on Israel.

In addition to the nearby Golan Heights, these mountains will largely be where the attackers' corpses and their war machines will fall. Habakkuk 2:17, in dealing with lead-up events to the day of the Lord, clarifies this: "The violence of Lebanon shall cover thee." Zechariah 11:1 declares, "Open thy doors, O Lebanon, that the fire may devour." And there's Isaiah 10:34, which refers to the great tribulation, "He shall cut down the thickets of the forest with iron, and Lebanon shall fall by a mighty one." Yet when the millennium is ushered in by Jesus, Israel shall "blossom as the rose" and the "glory of Lebanon shall be given unto it" (Is. 35:1-2).

War Breaks Out

Now back to Ezekiel 38:9, where we read that the Russians and their satellites "shall ascend and come like a storm, thou shalt be like a cloud to cover the land, thou, and all thy bands, and many people with thee." If the Israeli armies in the past Middle East wars, drawn from a population of three million or less, were able to repulse the armies from populations of a hundred million and more, is it conceivable that the Russians would take half measures in their assault on Israel?

Will the Western Europeans and the Americans just stay at home? Doesn't the United States have a mutual defense pact with Israel? Won't the insurgent Antichrist have already signed a peace covenant with Israel, ensuring the backing of his ten-nation federation? Things will be happening so fast they may find themselves unable to do little more than protest to the Russians and their satellites, "Art thou come to take a spoil? hast thou gathered thy company to take a prey? to carry away silver and gold...and goods, to take a great spoil?" (Ezek. 38:13).

But immediately "it shall come to pass at the same time when Gog shall come against the land of Israel, saith the Lord God, that my fury shall come up in my face. For in my jealousy and in the fire of my wrath have I spoken, surely in that day there shall be a great shaking in the land of Israel" (38:18-19). And God will see to it that He rains upon "him, and upon his bands, and upon the many people that are with him, an overflowing rain, and great hailstones, fire, and brimstone" (38:22).

God can do this by means of miracles utterly beyond our comprehension. Or He may choose that neutron bombs be used. We have already noted that the Israelis and the Soviets have no shortage of nuclear weaponry. Other countries, including Arab ones, either already have nuclear weapons or are acquiring them at a steady rate.

Victory Through Confusion

Could it be that God will repeat the pattern of 2 Chronicles 20, where King Jehoshaphat was attacked by three formidable enemies? Instead of Jehoshaphat having to fight, the foreign forces got so disoriented they killed each other.

A *Toronto Star* story about fourteen nations possessing "Nuclear Know-how" noted that three of those powers are Libya, Iraq and Iran. After the world has witnessed how blundering was Saddam Hussein's handling of his stockpiles of weaponry, one must frankly wonder if the Libyans, Ethiopians and Iranians, unable to handle their nuclear weaponry, will not fall into a tragic theater of the absurd and themselves inflict the release of nuclear death engines on the northern invaders.

James Dunnigan's *How to Make War* seems to indicate this possibility. He notes that in the Yom Kippur War the Arabs fired twenty-one hundred Soviet-made antiaircraft missiles. But of the eighty-five jets shot down, forty-five were their own.

We are given two specific clues in the Scriptures as to exactly what will happen in the Gog-Magog conflict. The first is that five-sixths of the Soviet army involved will perish on the mountains above Israel (Ezek. 39:2). The surviving one-sixth apparently will be turned back to go home and tell about it.

"And seven months shall the house of Israel be burying of them, that they may cleanse the land.... And there shall they bury Gog and all his multitude: and they shall call it the valley of Hamongog" (39:12,11). To "cleanse" apparently refers to burying the dead attackers and coping with the severe nuclear fallout and radioactive waste. Chernobyl is a reminder to us of what a colossal technical undertaking this will be. This scenario assumes a high survival rate for the Israelis, who will be able to tend to this task. And this is all the more reason to believe their defense will consist largely of neutron bombs, because they can be used surgically, destroying little more than human lives.

War and Rapture

The second specific clue is that the Soviets will have used equipment that leaves a surplus of fuel. The Israelis, frugal and fiercely practical as they are, will utilize this fuel for seven years: "And they that dwell in the cities of Israel shall go forth, and [utilize] the weapons [for fuel for]...seven years: so that they shall take no wood out of the field, neither cut down any out of the forests; for they shall [use the fuel of the] weapons" (39:9-10).

The Russians are known to have been making weapons out of a substance which is harder than steel but burns like wood. Its desirability is its immunity to radar detection. A Swedish bicycle has been produced that uses highly flammable plastic, and General Motors Corporation announced it could shortly be manufacturing car motors made exclusively of the same substance. Such developments may or may not be what is meant in Ezekial 39.

However, what is significant here may be the clue that this war will occur almost immediately after the rapture. Indeed, the rapture may trigger it. Why? Because the seven years the Israelis utilize the debris as fuel would coincide with the seven years of the great tribulation referred to by our Lord in Matthew 24:21.

The Americas, with their multitudes of born-again people suddenly raptured away from the distinguished posts of leadership which they occupy, would provide an opportune moment for the Soviets to make their move.

149

Of the half-billion born-again believers who would suddenly vacate earth in the rapture, about a hundred million would be from North America. And we can expect many North Americans will be missing from key political and defense positions, according to Christian educator Glen Greenwood. He estimates that in the 1990s the greatest concentration of American evangelical Christians per capita is in government, in Washington.

If this is true, what would hinder the Russians and their Islamic satellites from launching what Hitler called a "final solution" to the Jewish problem? What could anger the Soviets the most would be the Antichrist having signed a peace covenant with Israel. It would certainly rile the Libyans, Ethiopians, Iraqis and Iranians. This would result in the war we have just considered, in which Israel will prevail.

But the tragic point that affects the Soviet Union and, I fear, North America, is made in Ezekiel 39:6: "And I will send a fire on Magog, and among them that dwell carelessly in the isles [or "coastlands"]: and they shall know that I am the Lord." A very sobering possibility from this verse is that the successor to the Soviet Union may engage in an awful nuclear exchange with the United States.

Not only will there "be a great shaking in the land of Israel," but "all the men that are upon the face of the earth, shall shake" (Ezek. 38:19-20). It's the word "all" that cannot be ignored. Linking this passage with its parallels in Revelation, we see there will occur the first of the great earthquakes, which will cause mountains and islands to shift. Peoples universally will flee for cover to caves and mountains. With "the third part of men killed, by the fire [the nuclear bombs], and by the smoke [radiation, and the like]" (Rev. 9:18), many of these likely will be Russians and North Americans. To Russians God says, "I am against thee, O Gog" (Ezek. 39:1), if for nothing else than their imposition of atheism upon hundreds of millions of people for most of this century.

Only One Way Out

With the rapture having taken place, the North Americans left behind will be those who know they should have repented and turned to God but didn't. Revelation 9:20-21 describes them: "And the rest of the men which were not killed...repented not of the works of their hands, that they should not worship devils, and idols of gold, and silver, and brass, and stone, and of wood...neither repented they of their murders, nor of their sorceries, nor of their fornication, nor of their thefts."

The first nuclear conflict, in which "a third" die, is only a matter of when, not whether. "How shall we escape, if we neglect so great salvation" (Heb. 2:3)? There is no escape outside of Christ. Only those "in Christ" will be delivered from the wrath to come! It is precisely in this context that Paul promised, "God hath not appointed us to wrath, but to obtain salvation by our Lord Jesus Christ" (1 Thess. 5:9).

FIFTEEN

"ABOMINATION OF DESOLATION"

THE SCOT crisscrossed North America as if driven by a demonic obsession. In city after city Benjamin Creme went from radio studio to TV station to newspaper office to lecture theater. Professorial, pontifical and with a mesmerizing mystique, he was an announcer — a precursor, he said, of a christ who already is groomed and about to appear to the world.

Sixteen metropolitan newspapers — including *The New York Times*, the *Washington Post* and *The Los Angeles Times* — carried full-page ads announcing: "THE CHRIST IS NOW HERE." The text stated that "the world has had enough of hunger, injustice, war. Today Christians await the second coming. Jews await the Messiah, the Buddhists the fifth Buddha, the Muslims the Imam Mahdi, and the Hindus wait for Krishna. These are all names for one individual.... Look for a modern man concerned with modern problems — political, economic and social. [Shortly, this] christ (sic) will announce his identity.... From that time...we will build a new world."

A generation or two ago Creme would have been dismissed as a kook. The tragedy of the present world scene is that he is not.

He is, of course, not the only would-be savior of the world. Maharishi Mahesh Yogi, for example, tells his followers that he will be crowned king of the world. An expedient one too: He says that he will "save the world (in) one week maximum," according to a story in *The Toronto Star.*

Such vain posturings cannot but help the sincere Christian wonder whether to write off these would-be christs as the latest media-grabbing loons or to measure them against prophecy. We think of the words of Jesus: "I am come in my Father's name, and ye receive me not." But alas, "Another shall come in his own name, him ye will receive" (John 5:43).

When Jesus warned about the "abomination of desolation," He also inserted the command "whoso readeth, let him understand" (Matt. 24:15). Let us therefore examine the Scripture references that pertain to the Antichrist and the world scene that is becoming ripe for his unveiling.

"The Mystery of Iniquity"

Some of the most mysterious words Jesus ever uttered were: "Then shall the end come. When ye therefore shall see the abomination of desolation, spoken of by Daniel the prophet, stand in the holy place" (Matt. 24:14b-15).

Daniel wrote about the most evil man of all history leading the world into its most horrible holocaustic epoch. John's recording in the book of Revelation reads in many places as though it were half exposition of Daniel and half borrowed from today's most avant-garde science journals.

It was said that Hitler was called by many different names. Why? Because he was so evil. The Antichrist is called by many names — for the same reason. For starters, these names tell us much about him. Daniel referred to him as "the willful King," "the prince that shall come," "the King of fierce countenance" and "the little horn." John labels him "the beast," "666" and "the Antichrist"; and Paul calls him "the man of sin," "the son of perdition," "the man doomed to destruction" and "that wicked one."

Why is the Antichrist to be the most wicked man in all history? The answer is in his name: Antichrist — the very antithesis of Jesus Christ.

Jesus Christ is "the mystery of godliness" (1 Tim. 3:16); the Antichrist is "the mystery of iniquity" (2 Thess. 2:7). Jesus Christ is "the truth" (John 14:6); the Antichrist is the "lie" (2 Thess. 2:11). Jesus Christ came to save (Luke 19:10); the Antichrist, to destroy (Dan. 8:24). Jesus Christ is the "Good Shepherd" (John 10); the Antichrist, the evil shepherd (Zech. 11:16-17). Jesus Christ came in His Father's name; the Antichrist will come in his own (John 5:43). Jesus Christ came to do His Father's will (John 6:38); the Antichrist, his own will (Dan. 11:36). Jesus Christ humbled Himself (Phil. 2:8); the Antichrist exalts himself (2 Thess. 2:4). Jesus Christ was despised and afflicted (Is. 53); the Antichrist will be admired and lauded (Rev. 13:3-4). Jesus Christ was from heaven, to which He returned (John 6:38); the Antichrist from hell, to which he'll be sentenced (Rev. 20:10).

Emergence of Antichrist

The predictions of the actual Antichrist are hardly limited to religious circles. Hollywood's Harvey Bernhart was the producer of the trilogy of films *The Omen*, *Damien—Omen II* and *The Final Conflict*. He stated that *The Final Conflict* was an effort to capitalize on the universal fascination people have for the Antichrist. The lead character, Damien, is cast as a thirty-two-year-old business tycoon. Named United States ambassador to Britain, he goes on to coerce his way by guile and military conquest to become a world dictator. In the end he is overcome by the second coming of Christ.

To make the movie, Bernhart said he sought counsel from "Jess Moody, past president of 35,000 Baptist churches" and many Catholic clergy, according to a Canadian press report. Bernhart let it be known that, irreligious as he was, he found himself unable to "avoid a certain involvement when dealing with this subject.... But take a look at the disarray of the world today. It certainly is following what Revelation said. I think we are living awfully close to Armageddon now."

The Antichrist will emerge as a nice guy — someone who could write a book and outdo Dale Carnegie's *How to Win Friends and Influence People*. Yet Jesus intimated that he'll be the worst of wolves in sheep's clothing. Paul wrote that the "man of sin" would arrive on the scene with "power and signs and lying wonders" (2 Thess. 2:9), appearing as a minister of righteousness (2 Cor. 11:14-15).

Daniel 9 explains that when the times of the gentiles are complete, which I take to be the rapture of the church, the Antichrist will make his move and "confirm the covenant with [the Jews] for [one heptad, or period of seven years]. And in the midst of the [heptad] he shall cause the sacrifice and the oblation to cease, and for the overspreading of abominations he shall make it desolate, even until the consummation, and that determined shall be poured upon the desolate" (Dan. 9:27). Paul teaches, as I read it, that the Antichrist will not be revealed until this present age of the Holy Spirit is complete and the church is "taken out," or raptured (2 Thess. 2:6-8; 1 Thess. 4:16-18).

Europe Prepares the Way

Ripening Western Europe for the Antichrist's takeover, more than any single other factor, is spiritual apostasy. While millions are turning to Christ in Asia, Africa and the Americas, one seldom hears of such widespread awakenings in modern Western Europe. The evangelical congregations are tiny. The conventional churches are sparsely attended. The percentage of the population which professes to be born again is only a fraction of what it is in the Americas, Africa or east Asia.

The broadcast media there have been mysteriously closed to the gospel for two generations. *Church Around the World* says that "in thirty years of TV broadcasting, the people of France have never seen an evangelistic program."

Currently there are dramatic fulfillments of prophecy in Europe indicating the Antichrist could well be alive and in the wings, making ready for his revelation. For starters, the breaking away from the USSR of the former Soviet bloc countries during 1989-1991 had major prophetic implications. Many of these nations were members of the old Roman empire. They are seeking fraternity with Western Europe, though how they will fit in remains to be seen.

Originally Daniel's prophecy was made when he interpreted Nebuchadnezzar's dream of a metallic colossus bottoming out into the ten toes. Daniel indicated the toes represented ten nations at the end of secular history, emerging where the old Roman empire once stood.

Many Christian theologians have held to this interpretation. Jerome, one of the fathers of the Christian church, wrote sixteen hundred years ago, "All ecclesiastical authors have handed down that, in the consummation of the world, when the Kingdom of the Romans is destroyed, there will be ten rulers in the Roman world." Over a hundred years ago F.C. Bland wrote, "Ten kingdoms will be on the scene in the last days, the kingdoms designated by the ten toes of the image and by the ten horns of the Beast in Daniel." Robert Middleton wrote seventy-five years ago, when it couldn't have seemed more unlikely, that the Antichrist "will have the international federated army of the United States of Europe at his command, the military might of ten great powers."

Men as disparate as Friedrich Nietzsche, Aristotle Briand, Winston Churchill and John F. Kennedy dreamed of such a European confederacy. Richard Gwyn in London wrote in the September 2, 1990, *Toronto Star*, "The 1990s [must be thought of as] Europe's decade [when] the European community would evolve into the world's largest economic [and] political union." It seems incredible, but by 1986 West Germany, with less than a quarter of the population of the United States, had emerged as the world's largest exporter, according to the International Monetary Fund.

In 1972 the original six nations of the confederacy became nine, with the intent of stabilizing with ten "inner circle" members. The next step was that the European Economic Community (ECC) formed a parliament with 410 members, thereby going into the 1980s with a political infrastructure. During the 1980s the ECC was joined by Greece, Spain and Portugal, bringing its number up to twelve.

The first president of the ECC Parliament was Jewish — Simone Veil, an Auschwitz survivor with fierce allegiance to Israel. I recall vividly the newscaster on the CKO-Radio network remarking that the president could be thought of as a sort of "political messiah."

A later president of the ECC, Jacques Delors, remarked in 1990 that progress toward political union had far exceeded all expectations and that the realization of their goal was now inevitable. "We really have a rendezvous with destiny," he said. Scarcely did he know just how significant this observation would prove to be. The official organ of the ECC, *Europe Magazine*, contends regularly that the ECC must both politicize and militarize. Professor Robert Neild of Cambridge, director of the Stockholm International Peace Research Institute, observed in *The New York Times* that the countries of Western Europe are becoming increasingly wary of leaving their defense in the hands of the Americans and that there has never been such a groundswell of resolve to take responsibility for their own defense.

It is in this newly united Western Europe that the Antichrist will seize the reins and wield authority. His culmination of power may be precipitated by an economic collapse, a leadership vaccuum, a military foray or perhaps even a nuclear theater war.

A Time for Peace

The first augmentation of the Antichrist's power after the rapture of the church will be to sign a peace pact with a desperately questing Israel. Already, according to *Newsweek*, "The European Economic Community [has] undertaken a peace initiative in the Mideast." French president François Mitterand is much friendlier toward Israel than his predecessors D'Estang or De Gaulle. And this is also true of Britain's John Major. In a little-known effort during the 1970s, Israel sought membership in the ECC — more for military security than economic gain. Now Eric Moonman, a former ECC monitor, writes, "Israel should pursue its earlier application to become a member of the ECC."

Few objective observers could doubt that what Israel

craves most is peace and security on her borders. The first act by the Antichrist will be to sign a pact to meet that need.

Antichrist's Spiritual Foray

Jesus, Paul, John and Daniel all alluded to how the Antichrist would move from the political into the ecclesiastical arena, even becoming involved as an object of worship at the rebuilt temple. This is what Jesus referred to in His citation from Daniel, regarding the Antichrist standing in the holy place performing the "abomination of desolation." He turns from political protector to spiritual desecrater. "That man of sin [shall] be revealed, the son of perdition; who opposeth and exalteth himself above all that is called God, or that is worshipped; so that he as God sitteth in the temple of God, shewing himself that he is God" (2 Thess. 2:3-4).

We have looked at conjecture regarding the rebuilding of the temple. Will the Muslim Dome of the Rock sitting atop the old Solomon Temple foundation be blown up? Will it come down in an earthquake? Will it collapse in the holocaust — which some of us believe will take place, perhaps immediately after the rapture — when five-sixths of the Soviet army will be destroyed on the mountains from the Golan Heights northward?

Many think the temple will be built at the beginning of the millennium, after Armageddon, and that during the great tribulation the Jerusalem Great Synagogue now completed and located next to Hechal Shlomo (rabbinical headquarters) will be the scene of the "abomination of desolation." The two buildings share a common open plaza, large enough to accommodate an altar of sacrifice. There are a great number of Orthodox Jews who anticipate the reinstitution of animal sacrifice in the near future.

Thousands of Levites have been trained for this.

We have already seen how Russia and its Muslim allies will attack Israel. Once Russia is defeated, the Antichrist strikes out to conquer the world, which he orchestrates from Jerusalem. It is the midpoint in the seven-year tribulation — the latter half being, as Jesus called it, the "great tribulation, such as was not since the beginning of the world to this time, no, nor ever shall be" (Matt. 24:21).

Daniel 11:36-38 explains how the Antichrist will achieve his world conquest: "And the king shall do according to his will; and he shall exalt himself, and magnify himself above every god, and shall speak marvellous things against the God of gods, and shall prosper till the indignation be accomplished: for that that is determined shall be done. Neither shall he regard the God of his fathers, nor the desire of women, nor regard any god: for he shall magnify himself above all. But in his estate shall he honour the God of forces: and a god whom his fathers knew not shall he honour with gold, and silver, and with precious stones, and pleasant things."

One is hard-pressed to imagine the Antichrist literally conquering the world. Yet to look at nations individually, each has weaknesses which make it seem quite conceivable for the right figure to step in and bring unprecedented global unity.

India, for example, is depicted in *The Los Angeles Times* as a land of "mushrooming corruption, declining law and order, and growing public disquiet about the government's apparent inability to cope." The Antichrist will make short shrift there.

The [Willy] Brandt Commission on World Development reports that in the Third World, instead of an improvement, there has been further "deterioration." *The New York Times* states that many Third World leaders "advocate [a] New International Economic Order," something Bush and Gorbachev discussed at a 1990 summit; Canada's longtime ambassador for disarmament, Douglas Roche, also made a plea for the same in 1990.

While these problems are realistic enough, it still seems improbable that any one man could be vaulted to such heights of power that he could appear to solve them. In the flesh it could not occur. But, as we'll see next, the Antichrist will be empowered by Satan as no one before him has ever been.

SIXTEEN

THE REIGN
OF THE BEAST

AS WE'VE seen, songs glorifying Satan, death and God-hatred are becoming increasingly common in popular music. Add to this the Satan worship and devil emphasis in current novels and movies, and it's clear how conditioned the masses are becoming for a satanic dictator to take over. And what a takeover it will be. Under this ruler, born and bred of the occult, there will be attempts at total societal control that will dwarf anything the world has yet seen.

Hell-powered

Revelation 13:2-9 makes it clear how "the dragon [the devil] gave him [the Antichrist] his power, and his seat, and great authority. And I saw one of his heads as it were wounded to death; and his deadly wound was healed:...[the Antichrist dies and rises from the dead, and people were] saying, Who is like unto the beast? who is able to make war with him? And there was given unto him a mouth speaking great things and blasphemies; and power was given unto him to continue forty and two months. And he opened his mouth in blasphemy against

God, to blaspheme his name, and his tabernacle, and them that dwell in heaven. And it was given unto him to make war with the saints, and to overcome them: and power was given him over all kindreds, and tongues, and nations. And all that dwell upon the earth shall worship him, whose names are not written in the book of life of the Lamb slain from the foundation of the world. If any man have an ear, let him hear."

What an understatement: "If any man have an ear, let him hear"! Drugs are opening up the younger generation worldwide to demonization. As we have seen, pop culture is becoming ever more daring in brainwashing the young to worship the devil. The United States and Canada have never been thought of as countries dominated by the occult — but we need to take a new look.

A monstrous 666 in flaming Day-Glo, imprinted over a near-full-page black Star of David, was the cover display of a *Toronto Star* series on satanism, June 29-30, 1989. The articles described how "people blaming the prince of darkness have been implicated in more than a dozen crimes in southern Ontario ranging from the desecration of cemeteries to grisly murders." Police and cult experts in Canada and the United States are seeing an increased interest and participation in the beliefs and practices of satanism. Many satanists follow *The Satanic Bible*, by Anton Szandor LaVey, which advocates indulging to the hilt in the "seven deadly sins" of greed, pride, envy, anger, gluttony, lust and sloth.

One indicator that satanism is being taken seriously in modern society was ABC-TV's "20-20" showing on April 5, 1991, of an exorcism that took place in a New York church.

The broader movement on which satanism is piggybacking in North America is New Age. It is championed by such a high-profile figure as Shirley MacLaine. New

Age incorporates those who chart their lives on channeling, astrology, ESP, UFOs, reincarnation, transcendental meditation, Eastern religion and just about any other practice or philosophy in or out of the mainstream. All of them, being idolatrous, create an open door for Satan.

The Toronto Star reported that at the time of their "harmonic convergence," when the worldwide media focused on the New Agers, their fully committed numbers topped five million, with as many as a hundred million dabbling among their bizarre range of offerings. Various upscale New Age movements have infiltrated major corporations in the United States with their self-improvement programs.

Time says the number of New Age books increased tenfold in the past decade. The number of New Age bookstores has doubled in the past five years to about twenty-five hundred. New Age radio is proliferating. The Grammies now include a special prize for New Age music. A surprising number of successful stockbrokers consult astrological charts.

A Band of Evil

As a bishop often has an auxiliary bishop, the Antichrist will have an auxiliary. Revelation 13:11-13 says, "And I beheld another [the word means another of a similar kind] beast coming up out of the earth; and he had two horns like a lamb, and he spake as a dragon. And he exerciseth all the power of the first beast before him, and causeth the earth and them which dwell therein to worship the first beast, whose deadly wound was healed. And he doeth great wonders, so that he maketh fire come down from heaven on the earth in the sight of men."

The devil has always been an imitator. Here we see him counterfeiting the triune God — Father, Son and Holy

Spirit—with himself, as the dragon, corresponding to the Father; the Antichrist simulating Jesus Christ, wounded, dead and resurrected, at which time his powers become supernatural to a new degree; and the false prophet, who copies the Holy Spirit. This second beast focuses attention on the first beast, the Antichrist.

Revelation 13:13-15 describes how for forty-two months the false prophet seizes supernatural power and in the sight of men (probably through satellite TV) "deceiveth them that dwell on the earth by the means of those miracles which he had power to do in the sight of the beast; saying to them that dwell on the earth, that they should make an image to the beast, which had the wound by a sword, and did live. And he had power to give life unto the image of the beast, that the image of the beast should both speak, and cause that as many as would not worship the image of the beast should be killed."

A Master Manipulator

Self-styled messianic precursor Benjamin Creme, mentioned in the last chapter, says in his advertisement that when the coming "christ"—the Bible calls him the Antichrist—arrives, he will not emerge as a religious leader "but as a superman: mentally, physically and psychologically. He'll appear as the master of wisdom." His grasp of world problems and his knack for proposing solutions will set him apart from all other humans. "One day soon, men and women all over the world will gather around their radio and television sets to see and hear the christ: to see his face, and to hear his words dropping into their minds—in their own language." It's not mere allegiance but actual worship which the Antichrist will elicit.

Therefore the false prophet causes man to worship the Antichrist, including a huge image to the beast, which might well be the medium over which all world television programming is shown. Fyodor Dostoyevski was right to insist that men universally are creatures prone to worship.

And what power an image can generate! I was watching on TV a Halloween appeal program showing poor African children looking up at a big image of UNICEF, a United Nations organization, with the moving music and lyric, "The only friend they have is UNICEF." That's a tiny reflection of the kind of focus that will be directed toward the Antichrist. Commentator Clement Rogers bemoans, "Life has become so complicated that world government cannot be carried on by one man unless he is omnipresent." The Antichrist can have that kind of presence through television.

He can expect excellent cooperation from those working in the media. A *Chicago Tribune* poll found that whereas 42 percent of Americans go to church or a synagogue, only 8 percent of the media people do. In other words, the media workers tend to be more than five times as irreligious as the general public. Billy Graham has said that the president of a major TV network wields more power than the U.S. president.

As the Antichrist tightens his grip on the world, he will become more and more totalitarian. The chameleon of the ages, he'll have turned from peace promoter to warmonger; from fraternizing friend to fierce foe; from human advocate to superhuman adversary, as he unsheaths his sword with a worldwide vengeance. And he'll have all the modern mechanisms and electronics at his disposal.

Bert Raphael, chairman of the Canadian Lawyers and Jurists for Soviet Jewry, wrote in *The Toronto Star*, "The point our leaders continue to miss is that with the ever-shrinking number of democracies in the world, there may soon be no one left to protest." The Antichrist will not tolerate a million marchers in Europe — or anywhere —

against his regime. The *Toronto Sun* is unwittingly prophetic in foreseeing "a time in the future when no one questions the dictator" and reprisals "will be ubiquitous." He'll back his moves with immediate military force. *Time* could have been alluding to the future Antichrist when it observed, "Napoleon was correct when he declared that morality belongs to the country with the largest artillery." Of course, the Antichrist won't have forewarned the intellectual communities of the West of his intentions.

A Turn of Events

This leads to a grim period of austerity. There are so many passages on this, both in the Old Testament and the New. Revelation 6:15-16 says: "The kings of the earth, and the great men, and the rich men, and the chief captains, and the mighty men, and every bondman, and every free man, hid themselves in the dens and in the rocks of the mountains; and said to the mountains and rocks, Fall on us, and hide us from the face of him that sitteth on the throne, and from the wrath of the Lamb: for the great day of his wrath is come; and who shall be able to stand?"

The masses under the suppression of a ruthless dictator have always hated it, but what can they do? Senior citizen Sofia Berchanowski arrived in Toronto from Eastern Europe prior to the 1989 collapse of the Iron Curtain. She described how for the past generation millions — held under the hard heel of Marxist dictatorships — had simply sunk "into listless despair when military rule was imposed. People just stay quiet — they pray for God to help them. They walk around the streets with their faces long and thin. My relatives pray to die, instead of living in this situation."

This sounds like what Jesus described in His depiction of what life would be like when "the abomination of desolation" was established for forty-two months in the great tribulation: "Then let them which be in Judaea flee into the mountains: let him which is on the housetop not come down to take anything out of his house: neither let him which is in the field return back to take his clothes. And woe unto them that are with child, and to them that give suck in those days! But pray ye that your flight be not in the winter, neither on the sabbath day: for then shall be great tribulation, such as was not since the beginning of the world" (Matt. 24:16-21).

Reach Out and Mark Someone

It's one thing for the people of the world to see the Antichrist on TV or hear him on the radio. It's another thing for him to see them and to impose total control over them — to touch their lives tangibly. Revelation 13:16-18 characterizes the regime of the Antichrist when "he causeth all, both small and great, rich and poor, free and bond, to receive a mark in their right hand, or in their foreheads: and that no man might buy or sell, save he that had the mark, or the name of the beast, or the number of his name. Here is wisdom. Let him that hath understanding count the number of the beast: for it is the number of a man; and his number is Six hundred threescore and six."

More than a hundred years ago philanthropist Cecil Rhodes predicted, "In one hundred years all the world trade will be conducted by one man." His prophecy may be about to come true. Jacques Delors, president of the ECC, says the ECC nations will have one central bank beginning in 1993. Already the common currency of the ECC, the ECU (European Currency Unit), is being minted. This is especially significant because it is in Europe that the Antichrist will emerge.

For years there has been speculation about whether an omnipresent "Big Brother," as George Orwell wrote about, will arise, able to simplify increasingly complex problems in a diverse society. We may be close to seeing Big Brother in the guise of a computer network under the command of Antichrist.

Alix Granger's *Don't Bank on It* contends that today's "ubiquitous computer...will change banking more in the next five years than it has changed in the last hundred." First came the explosion worldwide of automated teller machines. Then world banking introduced the Electronic Funds Transfer System, whereby each customer is issued with a credit card, but which will gradually be replaced by a debit card (which deducts purchases directly from an account). The wave of the future is to eliminate all other cards and get us down to one plastic card on which will appear the equivalent of the individual's social security number (in the U.S.) or social insurance number (in Canada).

When the Antichrist takes over, cash as we know it will likely be eliminated. Employers will not issue paychecks to workers. Their wages will have been placed automatically in their accounts.

The business editor of the *Toronto Sun*, Garth Turner, explains that it is now being planned that a worldwide politico-economic central control bureau will have imbedded in every hand or forehead a chip to identify the carrier of a POS (point of sale) debit cardholder. Certainly most of us have had an invisible ink stamp imposed on our hand at amusement parks so we could go in and out unobstructed, the scanner picking up whether or not we had paid. Such developments are surely a precursor of the "mark of the beast."

No Turning Back

The Antichrist will press every frontier to impose his total control. Violators will pay with their lives. As we'll note in the next chapter, the martyrs will be in the millions; the human slaughter, in the billions. It will be, as Jesus assured us, the lowest level to which the world has ever sunk. The masses will be abysmally unhappy, but until worldwide issues swell to Armageddon itself, those who survive will have to bite the bullet.

SEVENTEEN

APPOINTMENT WITH ARMAGEDDON

THE LAST chapter showed how the Antichrist will achieve unprecedented worldwide power. He will claim to have the answers that no one else has to global problems. Many nations will submit to his leadership. Many peoples will worship him.

Yet this ruler's false utopia will be short-lived. During his reign, as Billy Graham expresses it, "tensions will mount, and once again the world will explode — with a gigantic world war of overwhelming ferocity involving conflict and massacre on an unparalleled scale. Even the iron grip of the Antichrist will be unable to prevent it. This massive upheaval will be the world's last war — the Battle of Armageddon."

Armageddon will be the place where the Antichrist will confront the kings of the earth for the final battle of mankind. Even the glib-tongued Antichrist cannot avert the world from this conflagration. In addition to what we have already seen in prophecy about this war, there is more to be learned about it from Scripture.

The Armageddon Schedule

We cannot predict the year Armageddon will occur, but the Bible gives many leads as to other aspects of its timing. In both Daniel and Revelation it's clear that the tribulation is divided into two parts, three and a half years each. Revelation 12:14 speaks of "time, and times, and half a time"; in 11:2 and 13:5 of the forty-two months; and in 11:3 and 12:6 of 1,260 days — which on the Jewish calendar is three and a half years. This period Jesus designated as the great tribulation.

Paul prophesied that "in the last days" the world would "wax worse and worse" (2 Tim. 3:1,13). Jesus forecast the same with regard to the great tribulation. Nature will convulse, and "there shall be signs in the sun, and in the moon, and in the stars; and upon the earth distress of nations, with perplexity; the sea and the waves roaring; men's hearts failing them for fear, and for looking after those things which are coming on the earth: for the powers of heaven shall be shaken. And then shall they see the Son of man coming in a cloud with power and great glory" (Luke 21:25-27).

Jesus said many things about Jerusalem, in particular, and the Middle East, in general, at the time of the end. There will be huge armies surrounding Jerusalem. Then it will be beleaguered, besieged and overrun. The earth will rock as if the land were riding ocean waves; people will think they are living on a giant water bed. The sun, moon and stars will black out. Crazed mobs will flee to the mountains. The powers of the heaven will be shaken with what would appear to be nuclear warfare. Myriads will drop dead from heart failure. During this last half of the tribulation people will enter a depression unprecedented in the history of mankind.

Opposition to the Antichrist

In the midst of this turmoil the Antichrist will not have the two-fisted grip on the world that he'd like to have. He'll be walking on logs in a roaring river, red with human blood. There will be regional mutiny from four blocs of the nations, as indicated by several passages.

Daniel 11:40 says that "at the time of the end shall the king of the south push at him." In verse 41 the Antichrist is in "the glorious land, and many countries shall be overthrown." And in verse 42, "He shall stretch forth his hand also upon the countries: and the land of Egypt shall not escape." These countries will roughly coincide with the Arab bloc of forty-one nations and the Organization of African Unity, formed in Ethiopia in 1963. Black African countries have continued their near-total isolation of Israel to show their support for the Arab bloc following the 1973 Middle East War, according to an Associated Press article.

In addition to the bloc of nations in the West — which is, of course, the Antichrist's original kingdom — and then the Arab/African bloc to the south, there's the bloc to the north. Daniel 11:40 states that the ruler of "the north shall come against him like a whirlwind...and with many ships." The Soviets will have undergone that earlier nuclear destruction in which five-sixths of their attacking armies were slain. And great nuclear destruction will have been wrought on their cities and their satellites. After five or six years, they're seeking revenge. We read that they "enter into the countries, and shall overflow and pass over" (v. 40). What a description of land, sea and air forces!

But there's one other section of the world to account for — the East. Daniel 11:44 says that "tidings out of the east...shall trouble him: therefore he shall go forth with

great fury to destroy, and utterly to make away many."
Revelation 9:16 says this bloc of nations to the east is a
mobilized army of 200 million. The most likely force to
come out of the east, crossing the Euphrates to get at
Israel, then to be ruled by the Antichrist, would seem to
be the non-Arabic Muslims. This group numbers 850
million and is increasing more rapidly than any other
religious body.

It would be awesome, yet entirely feasible, for the
Sword of Islam to draw two hundred million from the
Muslim populations of Iran, Afghanistan, Pakistan, India
and Indonesia. Many more than that have journeyed to
Mecca for religious reasons. War on behalf of Allah is a
religious imperative for Muslims.

Islam would fight anything Israeli at the drop of a hat.
It is feasible to conclude that Islam will be at the forefront.
Supporting this view is the fact that Muslims have control
over a huge dam in Turkey. By closing off a series of locks
they can dry up the Euphrates. Would the Turks do this to
clear a path for an oncoming army of fellow Muslims? It
would be their religious responsibility to do so.

On the other hand, there are many Bible students who
think a yet-unforeseen scenario will draw two hundred
million marchers from, say, Japan, India and China.
Stated the late Mao Tse Tung: "In the battle for the world,
China will field an army of 200 million." He told Henry
Kissinger in the 1970s that America simply must build a
bulwark of defense against the Soviets, whom the Chinese trusted not at all.

In the West many liberals have felt that if we just settle
down with the Soviets, through cooperation and coexis-
tence, we'll survive nicely. The Chinese do not share this
rose-tinted optimism. They contend that the greatest concentration of nuclear weaponry is in the Black Sea area,
ready to move against them. The present Chinese posture

toward the Soviets reflects what could be their posture in refusing to knuckle under to the Antichrist, and so they could well be the two hundred million rising up in rebellion against his monstrous regime.

Under the oppression of the Antichrist alignments will shift for pragmatic reasons, as peoples of differing ideologies join together to take on a common foe. India, Japan, the Philippines and the whole of the Far East could be banded together.

We should expect such developments because Scripture assures us repeatedly that "all nations" will assemble for Armageddon. Zechariah 14:1-3 says, "Behold, the day of the Lord cometh, and...I will gather all nations against Jerusalem to battle; and the city shall be taken...then shall the Lord go forth, and fight against those nations." Pope John Paul II uses the prophecy from Joel 2:1-2; 3:2,14 in his homilies: "The day of the Lord cometh...a day of darkness and of gloominess, a day of clouds and of thick darkness.... I will also gather all nations, and will bring them down into the valley of Jehoshaphat...multitudes, multitudes in the valley of decision: for the day of the Lord is near in the valley of decision."

The Supernatural Influence

Revelation 16:14 speaks of the false prophet, examined in the last chapter, working all kinds of occult miracles: "The spirits of devils, working miracles, which go forth unto the kings of...the whole world, to gather them to the battle of that great day of God Almighty." Billy Graham said in 1990, "I believe there are supernatural influences taking place" that will spur man to Armageddon. Principal J.S. Wright of Tyndale Hall, University of Bristol, points out that the Greek word *pharmakos* — as well as words derived from it, translated "sorcerer,"

175

"sorcery" and "witchcraft" in Scripture — carries "the root idea of drugs, potions, poisons" (Rev. 9:21; 21:8; 22:15 and Gal. 5:20). Passages such as Revelation 18:23, "By [Babylon's] sorceries were all nations deceived," indicate it could well be the drug pandemic that will have much to do with inciting the world to Armageddon.

The former director of the U.S. national drug control policy, William Bennett, said in the February 11, 1991, issue of *Christianity Today*, "I believe with Harvard psychiatrist Robert Colas that drugs are fundamentally a spiritual problem.... When people take drugs, they get a feeling of transcendence, of power, of control. That's a great deception...if drugs aren't a sin and if this isn't a form of idolatry, I don't know what it is."

It's not just rock stars, the ghetto poor and carefree students who make up the drug culture. Damaging drugs in various forms have spread throughout much of the world, as Milton Silverman has shown in *Prescriptions for Death: The Drugging of the Third World*. And even in the high echelons of society leaders are increasingly likely to be on drugs. It has become routine for American political or judicial candidates to acknowledge past marijuana use, and scandals have revealed that some already in office use drugs. These are some of the world leaders who will steer their peoples to Armageddon.

Pinpointing Armageddon

Does Armageddon, as a geographical site, exist? It does indeed! It is a fourteen-by-twenty-mile plain in northern Israel, stretching eastward from the foot of Mount Carmel, where Elijah invoked the fire of God to fall from heaven. Armageddon is at the crossroads of Israel, which is the land bridge between the three most populated continents on earth — Europe, Africa and Asia.

Napoleon, thought by many to have been the foremost military strategist in modern history, conquered part of Palestine in early 1799. As he gazed across this plain on a sunny day, he said, "[It's] the most natural battleground of the whole earth." Previous to Napoleon, Richard the Lion-Hearted of England, Louis of France, Pompey and Titus of Rome, Rameses of Egypt, Sargon, Sennacherib, Nebuchadnezzar, Antiochus Epiphanes and David had all fought wars at the site of Armageddon!

But will Armageddon be large enough to accommodate the congregating armies for the battle of Armageddon? No. As Joel prophesies, there'll be multitudes in the Valley of Jehoshaphat and throughout — and beyond — the Jordan Valley. And they'll be in Jerusalem. With millions overrunning the length and breadth of Israel, they'll overflow into what is now Lebanon, Syria, Jordan and the Sinai.

Everywhere there will be fighting to the death between these demonized, death-defying, bloodletting hordes and the Satan-possessed forces of the Antichrist. The slaughter! The carnage! The Bible says there will be pools of blood reaching as high as a horse's bridle. Jesus said there would be nothing like it in the annals of man.

Boston Globe columnist Ellen Goodman notes, "With monotonous regularity, the public rates nuclear war as its No. 1 concern. A full one-half of Americans surveyed believe that nuclear war will happen in their lifetimes." Those worrying may do so with good reason. Their proportion matches up with the fatalities that can be expected if the initial nuclear exchange that leads to Armageddon strikes soon.

Theologian Lehman Strauss calculates that six hundred million people are known to have been killed in wars throughout history. During the tribulation, if it were to occur in the 1990s, you could triple that number in the very first nuclear exchange, where one-third of the earth's population is wiped out (nearly two billion people). Another quarter of those surviving will be killed later, which means a total of half are slaughtered.

And what about those who survive till the final battle of Armageddon? Jesus said, "Except those days should be shortened, there should no flesh be saved: but for the elect's sake those days shall be shortened" (Matt. 24:22).

When Armageddon approaches, all thought of detente, SALT agreements and nuclear freeze will be flung to the winds. Nuclear winter will descend as a black blanket over whole sections of the earth. Man at his worst will uncork the whole bottle of lethal nuclear poison. Even John's description translated in King James English is vivid: "The seventh angel poured out his vial into the air...and there...[were] thunders, and lightnings; and there was a great earthquake [this could be seismic or nuclear-induced], such as was not since men were upon the earth, so mighty an earthquake, and so great." And such was the effect on the earth's crust that "every island fled away, and the mountains were not found. And there fell upon men [destruction] out of heaven" (Rev. 16:17-18,20-21).

There are several passages in the Old and New Testaments that say the sun ceases shining and the moon turns to blood. What's implied here is that the atmosphere is so polluted with the effects of nuclear explosions that the sun ceases to shine through — the moon and stars being virtually blanked out. As scientists have demonstrated, such effects would easily be wrought if all the submarines unleashed their nuclear arsenals, the air forces of the world dropped all their stockpiled bombs, and all the short-range, middle and intercontinental ballistic missiles were triggered. It used to be that students of Bible prophecy couldn't conceive of anything earthly that God could use to fulfill such prophecies. Today man is tangibly armed for Armageddon many times over.

Riding to the Rescue

The late Albert Schweitzer lamented, "Man has lost the capacity to foresee and to forestall; he will end by destroying the earth." Russell Clark expressed similar feelings in *The Toronto Star*: "I am a veteran of World War II, and well remember August 1945. Since that time I have lived with a feeling of near certainty that I would, indeed, see the end of civilization during my lifetime. The feeling has grown stronger and more pervasive in recent years, and I have really wondered whether there is any possible way out, short of a direct intervention by God."

There's good news for Clark: God does enter the scene. As Jesus promised, "As the lightning cometh out of the east, and shineth even unto the west; so shall also the coming of the Son of man be" (Matt. 24:27). Jesus Christ is going to step in and implement His own program of peace and prosperity. It is He who will terminate Armageddon before it exterminates the human race.

The passages illustrating Christ's intervention are many — Matthew 24, Mark 13, Luke 21, 2 Thessalonians 2 and Zechariah 14. Revelation 19:11 is particularly descriptive: "And I saw heaven opened, and behold a white horse; and he that sat upon him was called Faithful and True." Some prophetic students insist that armies will ride to Armageddon on horses. Will this white horse from heaven be a white Clydesdale, or a white quarter horse — born and bred in Kentucky and brought up on bluegrass? Of course not!

Bible writers, while literalists wherever possible, occasionally had to use the best language at their command to describe future events far removed from the technology of their own times. Consequently, we know Jesus Christ is the Man on the white horse. It was interesting to hear Johnny Carson ask one evening, "Is the man in the White House the man on the White Horse?" Of course he is not. Jesus Christ is! The Man on the white horse is called "Faithful and True, and in righteousness he doth judge and make war. His eyes were as a flame of fire, and on his head were many crowns; and he had a name written, that no man knew, but he himself. And he was clothed with a vesture dipped in blood: and his name is called The Word of God. And the armies which were in heaven followed him upon white horses, clothed in fine linen, white and clean. And out of his mouth goeth a sharp sword, that with it he should smite the nations" (Rev. 19:11-15).

Is that sword a multiple-podded laser beam? Enriched plutonium? An emission of nuclear or neutron bombs? Only God knows. What Scripture does teach is that God is a consuming fire — just as He is light. And He is love! "And he shall rule [the nations] with a rod of iron" (Rev. 2:27). This means He'll reign over the world with the total authority that encompasses His compassion.

So what happens to the chief villain in this story? Paul foretells about the Antichrist's body; John, about the total person. Our "Lord shall consume [him] with the spirit of his mouth, and shall destroy [him] with the brightness of his coming" (2 Thess. 2:8). John saw the Antichrist "and the kings of the earth, and their armies, gathered together to make war against him that sat on the horse, and against his army." And the Antichrist was "cast alive into a lake of fire burning with brimstone" (Rev. 19:19-20).

Jesus Christ baptizes the world with fire, as John the Baptist announced that He would. He judges the nations, as recorded in Matthew 25, and ushers in the millennium. History rises to its highest point ever as Jesus sets up His kingdom of peace and prosperity, with Jerusalem as its capital.

And, as Paul taught, the surviving Jews (as a nation) accept their Messiah. Zechariah foretold of the result of Armageddon: "And I will pour upon the house of David, and upon the inhabitants of Jerusalem, the spirit of grace and of supplications: and they shall look upon me whom they have pierced" (12:10). Yes, "and the Lord shall be king over all the earth: in that day shall there be one Lord, and his name one" (14:9). As Ezekiel put it, "One king shall be king to them all" (37:22).

When Jesus made His triumphant entry into Jerusalem, His followers hailed, "Hosannah to the king." But His time had not yet come. One week later a superscription hung over His cross in derision: "This is Jesus of Nazareth, the King of the Jews." He would be king, but not then, not until He came to turn Armageddon into a coronation.

At that point the saints will begin to live and reign "with Christ a thousand years" (Rev. 20:4). As we will see next, this special period will be unlike anything the world has ever seen.

EIGHTEEN

THE REIGN
OF KING JESUS

PRESIDENT BUSH, in his State of the Union address of January 29, 1991, described the coming new world order as one where "diverse nations are drawn together in a common cause to achieve peace." On March 5, amid the euphoria of an astounding triumph, the president exclaimed again before an ecstatic Congress that, yes, there's "a new world coming into view, a world in which there is a very real prospect of a new world order."

However, when the war was a month past, Bush conceded, "The victory over Iraq was not waged as 'a war to end all wars.' Even the new world order cannot guarantee an era of perpetual peace."

How right he was! As the war broke out *The Los Angeles Times* on January 18, 1991, commented that during our lifetime we've lived through five hundred wars. And at "any given time there are twenty-five border conflicts and usually thirty-five insurgencies." It predicted accurately, "There will be as many divisions and as much tension in the Mideast after we get out as there was before we went in. One of the most cherished illusions is that the United States can bring an end to the Arab-Israeli conflict."

As we will see, many people have sensed an era of peace, a secular version of the millennium, as being just around the corner. But the grim reality is that there is no reasonable hope of worldwide peace — if for no other reason than the fact that there is no rational expectation for an end to the Arab-Israeli conflict prior to Armageddon.

However, there is coming a true millennium, a period of one thousand years, in which Christ will reign in peace and prosperity. President Reagan boldly affirmed before the United Nations Second Special Session on Disarmament, "The Bible tells us there will be a time for peace." He was right. The millennial reign of the Messiah over the world is inevitable because God keeps His promises.

Counterfeit Millennia

"Ring out the thousand wars of old. Ring in the thousand years of peace." Engaging this quote from Alfred Lord Tennyson's "In Memoriam," Senator Ted Kennedy brought to a tumultuous climax the 1980 Democratic Party national convention. It was eloquent rhetoric, but man is incapable of ringing this bell.

Adolf Hitler's grandiose notion of Nazism was to aggrandize his imperialist regime into the entire earth. It would then last a thousand years. It didn't happen.

Time has cited Mao Tse Tung's "global export of revolution" to dominate the world of the future for a thousand years. Mao Tse Tung is dead, and so is his dream.

Soviet communism, too, was to be the inevitable wave of the future, burying democracy and capitalism in history's trash can. The Soviet Union has instead unravelled.

All these have proved to be pipe dreams. In perhaps the last great quest for a man-made millennium, the

Antichrist will speak of worldwide peace. For a brief period it will look as if finally the world will be consolidated under one dictator. It won't happen. As we have seen, the Antichrist's ascendancy will collapse in chaos after forty-two months (Rev. 13:5).

Jonathan Schell's "Bible" of the secular humanists, *The Fate of the Earth*, envisages, according to *Time*, a day when "existing institutions must give way to some sort of transcendent sovereignty and security, presumably by a government that embraces all mankind, in fact 'world government.' " That will happen, but only when Jesus Christ comes again! Only Christ can free humankind from terror, establish justice and effect peace. That new era will be the millennium.

Our Lord's prophetic words in Matthew 24 describe the great tribulation, which sinks man into a cataclysmic carnage, and the period to follow. "For there will be persecution such as the world has never before seen in all its history, and will never see again. In fact, unless those days are shortened, all mankind will perish. But they will be shortened for the sake of God's chosen people.... For as the lightning flashes across the sky from east to west, so shall my coming be, when I, the Messiah, return.... And the nations of the world will see me arrive in the clouds of heaven, with power and great glory. And I shall send forth my angels with the sound of a mighty trumpet blast, and they shall gather my chosen ones from the farthest ends of the earth and heaven (Matt. 24:21-22, 27, 30b-31, TLB).

Matthew 25 picks up the action: "When I, the Messiah, shall come in my glory, and all the angels with me, then I shall sit upon my throne of glory. And all the nations shall be gathered before me. And I will separate the people [or nations] as a shepherd separates the sheep from the goats, and place the sheep at my right hand, and the goats at my left. Then I, the King, shall say to those at my right, 'Come, blessed of my Father, into the Kingdom prepared for you from the founding of the world. For I was hungry and you fed me; I was thirsty and you gave me water; I was a stranger and you invited me into your homes; naked and you clothed me; sick and in prison, and you visited me' " (25:31-36, TLB).

First of all, note that it is the nations (v. 32) that Christ — now crowned king of the world — judges: nations that survive Armageddon. Their leaders have all come (Rev. 16:14). It will be history's foremost summit; only it will be summoned in a valley newly created by the all-time blockbuster earthquake. Zechariah says that the nations will stand before Him whose "feet will stand upon the Mount of Olives, to the east of Jerusalem, and the Mount of Olives will split apart, making a very wide valley running from east to west, for half the mountain will move toward the north and half toward the south" (Zech. 14:4, TLB).

This happens just prior to when "the Lord shall be King over all the earth. In that day there shall be one Lord — his name alone will be worshiped" (Zech. 14:9, TLB). There the judgment of the nations will take place. It will be based on how the nations have treated those of Israel who have received Christ as their Messiah, along with those redeemed and discipled by the 144,000 Jewish evangelists during the great tribulation. Of course, "two-thirds of all the nation of Israel will be cut off and die, but a third will be left in the land. I will bring the third that remain through the fire and make them pure, as gold and silver are refined and purified by fire. They will call upon my name and I will hear them; I will say, 'These are my people,' and they will say, 'The Lord is our God' " (Zech. 13:8-9, TLB). The "fire" refers to the tribulation and the holocausts, including Armageddon.

The hammer of history will have come down on the anvil at Armageddon. The crushing of the nations, at the beckoning of Christ, will determine who goes to hell and who goes into the millennial kingdom.

These will be joined at Christ's installation of the millennium by the newly resurrected tribulation saints (a sizable percentage of whom will be martyrs), along with the Old Testament believers up to the time of the church, who also will be resurrected at this time. The total church will also consist of those saints who come with Christ in His second coming. There is no scriptural basis that any of these groups will receive glorified bodies at this point. Rather they will be resurrected as Old Testament believers were on the occasion of Christ's resurrection. They will, however, live a thousand years, because Satan and the Adamic curse on nature will be removed.

In Revelation 20 John foresaw what would happen when Christ came back to earth and defeated the Antichrist at Armageddon. "Then I saw an angel come down from heaven with the key to the bottomless pit and a heavy chain in his hand. He seized the Dragon — that old Serpent, the devil, Satan — and bound him in chains for 1,000 years, and threw him into the bottomless pit, which he then shut and locked, so that he could not fool the nations....

"Then I saw thrones, and sitting on them were those who had been given the right to judge. [Author's note: These will be members of the church, who are in their glorified bodies.] And I saw the souls of those who had been beheaded for their testimony about Jesus, for proclaiming the Word of God, and who had not worshiped the Creature or his statue, nor accepted his mark on their foreheads or their hands. They had come to life again and now they reigned with Christ for a thousand years.

"This is the First Resurrection. (The rest of the dead

did not come back to life until the thousand years had ended.) Blessed and holy are those who share in the First Resurrection. For them the Second Death holds no terrors, for they will be priests of God and of Christ, and shall reign with him a thousand years" (Rev. 20:1-6, TLB).

The first resurrection refers to a "who" rather than a "when"; that is, those who are Christ's — from whatever era — are assumed to be included in His first resurrection. Those who are not Christ's will be resurrected to the great white throne judgment and sentenced to their eternal destiny (see Rev. 20:11-15).

For those of us who anticipate reigning as His bride and presiding with Christ for a thousand years over this earth, it could all begin as soon as seven years from now.

The Real Thing

Considering its importance, the millennium is certainly one of the least written-about and unpublicized of themes. Instead man invents plans for a utopia. Since Adam and Eve were ejected from the Garden of Eden, prophets, poets, musicians, political philosophers, theologians and artists have dreamed of an eventual golden age when — under the benevolent reign of an all-seeing, all-knowing, all-powerful ruler — one could live in harmony with his maker, family and society. Such dream schemes have proved to be just that — dream schemes.

Yet man keeps dreaming. On September 27, 1991, eight scientists (four single women and four single men) locked themselves into a glassed-in geodesic biosphere thirty miles north of Tucson, Arizona, for two years. They plan to experience what Texas billionaire Edward Bass, its financier, is calling the Garden of Eden restored.

The steel and glass compound houses thirty-eight hundred varieties of plants and animals. It was designed to provide the perfect environment for humans, surrounded as they are with biomaterial such as pot-bellied pigs, Tilapia fish and Pygmy goats (for milk). Staples include papayas and all kinds of vegetables. Contact with the outside world is limited to videocassette recorders, telephone and computer communications.

The experiment may prove interesting, but it's certainly not a microcosm for a peaceful world. Its results and successive experiments will not serve as blueprints for a true millennium because they still depend on man. Besides, God has a totally different plan.

What to Expect

The only accurate plan for a millennium is found in the Bible. God's Word assures us that a golden age lies just beyond Armageddon — an age of unprecedented peace and prosperity. This idyllic age will not be a democracy, a monarchy or a socialist state. It will be a theocracy. Christ will be Lord and King over all the earth. What the Antichrist will have failed to do with militaristic might and computer surveillance, Jesus Christ will do by His omniscience, omnipotence and omnipresence.

Isaiah prophesied: "The government shall be upon his shoulder. These will be his royal titles: 'Wonderful,' 'Counselor,' 'The Mighty God,' 'The Everlasting Father,' 'The Prince of Peace.' His ever-expanding, peaceful government will never end. He will rule with perfect fairness and justice from the throne of his father David. He will bring true justice and peace to all the nations of the world. This is going to happen because the Lord of heaven's armies has dedicated himself to do it!" (Is. 9:6-7, TLB).

At this time the angel's prophecy to Mary will be fulfilled: "And the Lord God shall give him the throne of

his ancestor David. And he shall reign over Israel forever;
his Kingdom shall never end" (Luke 1:32-33, TLB).
Christ will assume that throne to which he is legally
appointed by his Father (Matt. 1:20; Luke 1:27).

Israel, a tiny land, will be enlarged from the Nile to the
Euphrates, with the future regathering of Israel being
vastly expanded over what we've seen during the last one
hundred years. Today four and a half million of the
world's seventeen million Jews are in Israel. And what of
the "ten tribes"? God knows who and where they are and
just how He will arouse them to return. In the millennium
Israel will be divided according to the ancient twelve
tribes (Ezekiel 47-48 gives the precise divisions).

A Gathering of Peoples

All nations and peoples will worship King Jesus, God's
anointed One (Ps. 2:2). No longer will people take pil-
grimages to Washington, Rome, Moscow or Mecca. "In
the end, those who survive the plague will go up to
Jerusalem each year to worship the King, the Lord of
Hosts, to celebrate a time of thanksgiving. And any nation
anywhere in all the world that refuses to come to Jerusalem to worship the King, the Lord of Hosts, will have no
rain" (Zech. 14:16-17, TLB). And who will rule over the
flourishing twelve regions of Israel? Jesus replied,
"When I, the Messiah, shall sit upon my glorious throne
in the Kingdom, you my disciples shall certainly sit on
twelve thrones judging the twelve tribes of Israel" (Matt.
19:28, TLB).

When Christ comes again to set up His thousand-year
reign, His capital will be Jerusalem. With supra-metro-
politan Jerusalem as the capital, and a vastly expanded
Israel as the center of the earth, the millennium will be
resplendent. The world will flourish amid the worship

and service of Christ the King, as the Abrahamic covenant will be fully realized.

The worldwide dominion of our Lord will include the multitudinous tongues of the gentile nations (Amos 9:12; Micah 7:16-17; Zech. 14:16-19; Is. 66:18). There will be a total transformation of the geopolitical configuration, as prophesied in Isaiah, "In that day the Lord will make himself known to the Egyptians. Yes, they will know the Lord and give their sacrifices and offerings to him.... In that day Egypt and Iraq will be connected by a highway, and the Egyptians and the Iraqi will move freely back and forth between their lands, and they shall worship the same God. And Israel will be their ally; the three will be together, and Israel will be a blessing to them. For the Lord will bless Egypt and Iraq because of their friendship with Israel. He will say, 'Blessed be Egypt, my people; blessed be Iraq, the land I have made; blessed be Israel, my inheritance!' " (Is. 19:21,23-25, TLB).

Yes, even Egypt and Iraq! Only a miracle could bring about such a change, and that's exactly what the world is in store for.

On a statue across from the United Nations headquarters is the inscription: "They shall beat their swords into plowshares." That really will happen — in the millennium, when the Lord will rule the whole world from Jerusalem! Micah says, "He will issue his laws and announce his decrees from there. He will arbitrate among the nations, and dictate to strong nations far away. They will beat their swords into plowshares and their spears into pruning-hooks; nations shall no longer fight each other, for all war will end. There will be universal peace, and all the military academies and training camps will be closed down. Everyone will live quietly in his own home in peace and prosperity, for there will be nothing to fear. The Lord himself has promised this" (Micah 4:2-4, TLB).

Peter urged us to "love the brotherhood" (1 Pet. 2:17). The trouble with our world today is that we have more hoods than brothers — brothers meaning those who've been born again into God's kingdom. One day the true brotherhood of God will prevail. It will happen when Christ comes again to establish His kingdom. And so transformed will the world be that even the beasts will be tamed: "In that day the wolf and the lamb will lie down together, and the leopard and goats will be at peace. Calves and fat cattle will be safe among lions, and a little child shall lead them all. The cows will graze among bears; cubs and calves will lie down together, and lions will eat grass like the cows. Babies will crawl safely among poisonous snakes, and a little child who puts his hand in a nest of deadly adders will pull it out unharmed. Nothing will hurt or destroy in all my holy mountain, for as the waters fill the sea, so shall the earth be full of the knowledge of the Lord" (Is. 11:6-9, TLB).

Christ will remove all sickness, deformities and handicaps. There will be no blindness, deafness or dumbness; no need for eyeglasses, hearing aids, speech therapy, wheelchairs or crutches (Is. 29:18; 33:24; 35:3-6; Jer. 30:17; Ezek. 34:16).

Age as we know it will be altered. "The streets will be filled with boys and girls at play"; while with the world in a state of "peace and prosperity" there "will once again be aged men and women" (Zech. 8:4, TLB). Like Adam and Methuselah, perhaps the aged will live up to a thousand years old.

And how will the earth support such a flourishing, proliferating population? The Lord will remove the ancient curse upon agriculture (Gen. 3:18). Even "the wilderness and desert will rejoice in those days; the desert will blossom with flowers. Yes, there will be an abundance of flowers and singing and joy! The deserts will become as green as the Lebanon mountains, as lovely as Mount Carmel's pastures and Sharon's meadows; for the Lord will display his glory there, the excellency of our God" (Is. 35:1-2, TLB).

There will be no need for psychiatrists or "uppers" to lift people from depression. But of this present age Paul wrote, "Even we [as] Christians, although we have the Holy Spirit within us as a foretaste of future glory, also groan to be released from pain and suffering" (Rom. 8:23, TLB). "For all creation is waiting patiently and hopefully for that future day when God will resurrect his children. For on that day thorns and thistles, sin, death, and decay — the things that overcame the world against its will at God's command — will all disappear, and the world around us will share in the glorious freedom from sin which God's children enjoy. For we know that even the things of nature, like animals and plants, suffer in sickness and death as they await this great event" (Rom. 8:19-22, TLB).

For all of history man has yearned for such an era of perfect peace and prosperity. The wonderful assurance of God's Word is that it's coming.

NINETEEN

EVERLASTING FIRE

WHEN I was at Oxford University, C.S. Lewis told about going to hear a certain preacher. The young man ended his sermon by suggesting, "If you do not heed these words, there will be eschatological consequences."

Shaking hands with him at the church door, Lewis asked, "Did you mean that if your hearers didn't believe in Christ, they'd go to hell?"

"Yes," replied the young pastor.

"Then why didn't you tell them?" said Lewis.

The preacher's timid approach to judgment and hell is common in this day. For half a century liberal theologians have predicted that enlightened moderns would abandon belief in a literal hell. They were partially right. University of Chicago divinity professor Martin Marty, perhaps the best-known current chronicler of North American religious trends, conceded in a March 25, 1991, *U.S. News and World Report* article that, like many people, he doesn't believe there is a hell.

"If people really believed in hell, they wouldn't be watching basketball or even TV preachers," he said. "They'd be out rescuing people."

In contrast, professor Kenneth S. Kantzer of Trinity

Evangelical Divinity School in Deerfield, Illinois, and a former editor of *Christianity Today*, affirms, "The Bible makes it clear that hell is real" and that "consignment to hell means eternal separation from God, and that alone...is a horrendous punishment." Nevertheless, Kantzer, along with millions of other clergy, finds hell not an attractive subject to address. He confessed that he hadn't "preached a sermon on hell in more than three decades."

In the spring of 1991 pollster George Gallup reported that more North Americans currently believe in the reality of "hell than ever recorded before." Sixty percent said they believe there is a place to which the unrepentant who have led bad lives will be damned eternally.

In the final analysis it doesn't matter what the masses think. It doesn't matter what the experts think. What counts is what the Bible says because it is God's eternal law book. So in light of this study of the end times, we need to know from where and when and under what circumstances Christ-rejecters will be assigned and sentenced to eternal hell.

The old saying has it that "all good things must come to an end." Will the millennium end in triumph or tragedy — in jubilation or judgment? The answer is that it will — as have all other preceding eras of human history — end in a downer, a plunge that leads not only to tragedy but to the physical dissolution of the world and heavens around it, and straight on to the great white throne judgment. Let's see exactly what happens.

Great Balls of Fire

Revelation 20 says that Christ will have incarcerated Satan in "the bottomless pit...bound [and] in chains for 1,000 years...so that he could not fool the nations any more until the thousand years were finished. Afterwards he would be released again for a little while" (Rev. 20:2-3, TLB). John continued: "When the thousand years end, Satan will be let out of his prison. He will go out to deceive the nations of the world and gather them together, with Gog and Magog, for battle — a mighty host, numberless as sand along the shore. They will go up across the broad plain of the earth and surround God's people and the beloved city of Jerusalem on every side. But fire from God in heaven will flash down on the attacking armies and consume them" (Rev. 20:7-9, TLB).

Satan, Gog and Magog again? That's what John foresaw: There will be residual unbelief and rebellion throughout North-Central Euro-Asia in particular and the earth generally. It will surface during the final days of the millennium, as the "world and the flesh" — which will still be with us during the millennium — will be joined with satanic influences. This latent evil will be strengthened by a briefly released Satan, who will go berserk because he'll know his time is so short. Like the Judas he possessed to betray our Lord, what he does he will do quickly — very quickly!

This brings us to the ultimate conflagration of history. Peter wrote, "The day of the Lord is surely coming, as unexpectedly as a thief, and then the heavens will pass away with a terrible noise and the heavenly bodies will disappear in fire, and the earth and everything on it will be burned up. And so since everything around us is going to melt away, what holy, godly lives we should be living!.... God will set the heavens on fire, and the heavenly bodies will melt and disappear in flames" (2 Pet. 3:10-12, TLB).

Despite this mass destruction, we can look forward to "God's promise of new heavens and a new earth afterwards, where there will be only goodness" (2 Pet. 3:13, TLB).

Jesus alluded to the same thing in Matthew 24:35 (TLB): "Heaven and earth will disappear, but my words remain forever." Is the world to go up totally in nuclear flames at any time now? No. But it will eventually be consumed in some fashion, and with it the whole of the universe.

If the world's sixty-thousand hydrogen bombs were to go off at once, what would happen? Only God knows! We're told there's enough wreaking of death in sixty-thousand H-bombs to incinerate one hundred times over the world's five and a half billion people.

Milton Burton, an Oak Ridge nuclear scientist who helped produce the first atomic bomb, has said there exists the distinct possibility "of lighting the nitrogen chain, in which event the whole world would go up in flames." Burton went on to say, "Should other planets be inhabited, they would look and cry, 'Ah, a nova, a new star.' "

Such scenarios could be the beginning of the ultimate end of history as we know it. Whatever means God uses, the Bible tells us for sure that what will happen — more than a thousand years in the future — is that the whole physical universe will go up at once in flames.

Writer Gwynne Dyer reckons that with the weaponry available today, the world is doomed. Yet it may not be World War III that finishes everything off. It well "might take World War IV, or even World War V." Dyer may be correct — if World War III is the Russian/Muslim assault on Israel, and World War IV is Armageddon, then World War V must be thought of as the final war at the end of the millennium between Satan, with his reassembled forces, and those of Christ the King. At this point, Peter prophesied, not only the earth but the heavens will decompose in flames.

Scientists have postulated for years how the physical cosmos could collapse in a big bang-like consummation — based on the same principles upon which it allegedly came into existence at creation's dawn. If so, it would surely be the signal for the great white throne judgment!

Judgment Day

The book of Revelation describes this culmination of human history. In chapter 20 John records how Satan has seduced the residue of the rebellious in the millennial world, as concentrated in Gog and Magog, and "God in heaven will flash down on the attacking armies and consume them. Then the devil who had betrayed them will again be thrown into the Lake of Fire" where the Antichrist "...and False Prophet are, and they will be tormented day and night forever and ever" (Rev. 20:9-10). That's it! Satan will be gone forever!

Then John described the judgment before the great white throne: "And I saw a great white throne and the one who sat upon it, from whose face the earth and sky fled away, but they found no place to hide. I saw the dead, great and small, standing before God; and The Books were opened, including the Book of Life. And the dead were judged according to the things written in The Books, each according to the deeds he had done. The oceans surrendered the bodies buried in them; and the earth and the underworld gave up the dead in them. Each was judged according to his deeds. And Death and Hell were thrown into the Lake of Fire. This is the Second Death — the Lake of Fire. And if anyone's name was not found recorded in the Book of Life, he was thrown into the Lake of Fire" (Rev. 20:11-15, TLB).

Surely this was the consummation judgment to which Paul alluded when he urged the Athenians to repent, "because [God] hath appointed a day, in the which he will judge the world in righteousness by that man whom he hath ordained; whereof he hath given assurance unto all men, in that he hath raised him from the dead" (Acts 17:31).

Thomas Axworthy, Pierre Trudeau's longtime principal secretary, wrote in *Maclean's* that all political "leaders must answer to their Maker for their personal sins." How about the Hitlers and the Husseins? The *U.S. News and World Report* of March 25, 1991, noted that while Christians of diverse persuasions may differ widely on the details of judgment day and the consequent sentencing to hell, it is commonly felt "that some evils are 'so great that no punishment in this life can be adequate.' "

Jesus assured us they will get what's coming to them. To the impenitent He will say, "Away with you, you cursed ones, into the eternal fire prepared for the devil and his demons" and "they shall go away into eternal punishment" (Matt. 25:41,46, TLB). This is the "second death" to which John alludes in Revelation 20:14 and again in 21:8 (NIV): "But the cowardly, the unbelieving, the vile, the murderers, the sexually immoral, those who practice magic arts, the idolators and all liars — their place will be in the fiery lake of burning sulfur. This is the second death."

Is hell really that bad? General Sherman reckoned in the nineteenth century, "War is hell." If that was true then, what could be said today? During Desert Storm the main highway from Iraq into Kuwait was called "the road to hell." It wasn't. The so-called smart bombs, which did such devastating damage, were named hellfire bombs. But they were not even close to being hellfire! And

CNN's Bernard Shaw exclaimed as the first tracer bombs lit up the Baghdad sky on that unforgettable mid-January night, "Ladies and gentlemen, I've never been there, but it feels like we're in the center of hell." Wrong again. War puts an end to life. *Hell perpetuates existence in torment forever.*

The Reality of Hell

When the Pharisees asked Jesus when the kingdom of God would begin (Luke 17:20), He told them, "As the lightning, that lighteneth out of the one part under heaven...so shall also the Son of man be in his day" (Luke 17:24). Jesus said it would be "as it was in the days of Lot; they did eat, they drank, they bought, they sold, they planted, they builded; but the same day that Lot went out of Sodom it rained fire and brimstone from heaven, and destroyed them all. Even thus shall it be in the day when the Son of man is revealed." And then He gave that terribly solemn warning, "Remember Lot's wife" (Luke 17:28-30, 32).

Jesus was addressing people who were devoutly religious but who nevertheless rejected Him as Messiah. He warned them that just as a sudden and severe judgment came upon Sodom — and Lot's wife — so too another, larger, judgment is due for all mankind.

What few realize is that Jesus spoke thirteen times as much about hell as He did about heaven! Why did He do this? Because He is God and He knows the complete truth. He wants people, whom He loves so much that He came from the glories of heaven to die for them, to stay out of hellfire.

Jesus' reference to "fire and brimstone" and the warning to "remember Lot's wife" speak directly of the final judgment. The first atomic bomb killed one hundred thousand people in Hiroshima, Japan. Some who were fleeing Hiroshima and Nagasaki turned back to see the incomprehensible destruction, just as Lot's wife did as she fled Sodom. But, exposed to the nuclear explosion, the fleeing Japanese who turned to look back were turned into salt-like — or ashy — pillars resembling burnt, unsnuffed cigarettes!

The word Moses used for salt in Genesis 19:26, where Lot's wife became a pillar of salt, was also used in Deuteronomy 29:22-23. In this passage Moses warned of a future generation that would see "brimstone, and salt, and burning." So perhaps the pillar of salt may have actually resembled a pillar of ash more than a rock-like piece of salt. Jesus, in prophesying hellfire, may well have been referring to a form of fire and brimstone that was not the oxidation fire familiar to His earthly contemporaries. It was a kind of fire not known then, and perhaps not known yet. A combustion such as this — such as a nuclear holocaust — could fulfill end-time prophecies.

The connection between hell and fire is no mere figurative language. Jesus said those who reject Him would be "cast into hell, into the fire that never shall be quenched: where their worm dieth not, and the fire is not quenched" (Mark 9:45-46). Over and over again in Mark 9:43-48 Jesus spoke of the impenitent being cast into hell, where the fire is never quenched.

No Expiration Date on Eternity

In verse 49 Jesus added, "Every one shall be salted with fire." So what does salt do? Back on the farm in Saskatchewan we'd rub salt into hams — and they'd hang on the wall in the summer heat for weeks without spoiling. One of the truly hellish things about hell is that its inhabitants have been "salted" to last for eternity.

There are no return tickets from hell.

Jesus said hellfire is forever, yet its victims are preserved rather than consumed. No, we don't understand it any more than we understand how there can be intense fire in a place the Bible describes as outer darkness. I once put this to James Kennedy, pastor of Coral Ridge Presbyterian Church in Fort Lauderdale, Florida. He likened hell to a microwave oven which cooks its contents inside a cabinet where there's intense heat amidst total darkness. Most of us don't understand what is known about neutron bombs — that when detonated they destroy life while preserving property. Yet such weapons exist and may be waiting to play their role in that cavernous horror chamber which the Bible calls hell.

Do we understand how the visible heavens and earth will be burned up with fire, yet earth's inhabitants will be preserved by fire, to burn forever? Isaiah asked, "The sinners in Zion are afraid...who among us shall dwell with everlasting burnings?" (Is. 33:14) Next to the question "What then shall I do with Jesus who is called Christ?" the most important question a person can ask is, "Who among us shall dwell with everlasting burnings?" To those questions there is a sure answer, the only One who can calm fears of eternal damnation: Jesus Christ and the "so great salvation" (Heb. 2:3) He offers to all mankind. "There is no eternal doom awaiting those who trust him to save them" (John 3:18, TLB).

TWENTY

"I WILL COME AGAIN"

AL MAZEROLLE was fighting for the Allies at Normandy on D-Day, the historic turning point in World War II that led to the defeat of the Nazis. A little girl, Edith Bodin, had been shot by the fleeing Nazis and dropped in a ditch for dead. The bullet, perilously close to her heart, likely would have killed her had it not been for Mazerolle. He made a daring dash through bullets and exploding bombs to rescue Edith. Doctors operated on her. She survived.

Decades later, when a D-Day anniversary was being observed in Normandy, Mazerolle went to France from his home in British Columbia. Beautiful Edith Bodin, now middle-aged and never having seen him since she was a tiny girl, had tears streaming down her cheeks when she saw Mazerolle. Throwing her arms around the wizened old man, she exclaimed, "Savior!"

That one word said it all.

Paul, in a similar vein, wrote that believers in the risen Christ are "looking for that blessed hope, and the glorious appearing of the great God and our Saviour Jesus Christ" (Titus 2:13). Just as the old Canadian veteran returned to the scene of a one-time bloody battlefield to meet again with the one he had saved, who greeted him with the exclamation "Savior!" — so when Jesus Christ returns to evacuate us to be forever with Him, our response will be a euphoric "Savior!"

Missing or "Missiling"?

Leonard DuPree, a Plains, Georgia, native and a cousin of Jimmy Carter, told me that with the signs of the times as they are, one of his Southern black brothers said, "Gabriel must be licking his lips." He was speaking of the rapture, which precedes the tribulation, and how it will be announced by the angel Gabriel's blowing of the trump of God. One of these days, wrote Paul, "The trumpet shall sound, and the dead shall be raised incorruptible, and we shall be changed" (1 Cor. 15:52).

Paul was more explicit in 1 Thessalonians 4:15-18 (TLB): "I can tell you this directly from the Lord: that we who are still living when the Lord returns will not rise to meet him ahead of those who are in their graves. For the Lord himself will come down from heaven with a mighty shout and with the soul-stirring cry of the archangel and the great trumpet-call of God. And the believers who are dead will be the first to rise to meet the Lord. Then we who are still alive and remain on the earth will be caught up with them in the clouds to meet the Lord in the air and remain with him forever. So comfort and encourage each other with this news."

Christians can rejoice that 85,000 people daily give their lives to the Lord. Of these, 30,000 are in Africa, 25,000 in China and 5,000 in the Soviet Union. The *Church Around the World* points to such remarkable assemblies as the Yoido Full Gospel Church in Korea, pastored by Paul Yonggi Cho. It has a current congregation of 700,000 members and has been increasing its membership, on average, by 10,000 per month. According to the World Christian Encyclopedia, there are 550 million Christians in the world. So if Christ returned today, perhaps one in ten would rise from earth to be forever with the Lord.

Jesus said when He comes there will be countless beds from which one will be taken and the other left; fields in which one worker will be taken and the other left. When that day comes, will you be missing from the chosen or "missiling" heavenward, forever to be with Him?

The rapture is no far-out doctrine held by a tiny minority of fanatics. According to *Christianity Today* (April 29, 1991), "The pretribulation and premillennial positions — that is, the views that maintain Christians will be 'raptured' before the tribulation [have] been accepted by...the majority of evangelicals." Polling its readership for their views, it discovered that those who believe Jesus will come before the millennium outnumber those who subscribe to all other views combined, including those with no opinion, by a three to two margin. When asked, Do you think all (Bible) prophecy should be interpreted literally? those who said yes outnumbered those who said no, ten to seven. It was concluded that "pretribulational-premillennialism" must be considered "the dominant eschatological position among evangelicals today." Over three-quarters of the magazine's readers believed that their views on Christ's return are important to the way they live their Christian lives.

When Billy Graham visited the Baptist church in Moscow, there had to be five consecutive services to accommodate the crowds. Their primary interest was the second coming of Jesus Christ. Whenever Graham visited the White House during President Reagan's tenure there,

Reagan would ask him as his guest preacher to speak on the second coming. At all levels of society people hunger to know more of this doctrine.

A Happy Ending

After one warning of coming persecution, Jesus consoled His disciples: "Let not your heart be troubled: ye believe in God, believe also in me. In my Father's house are many mansions: if it were not so, I would have told you. I go to prepare a place for you. And if I go and prepare a place for you, I will come again, and receive you unto myself; that where I am, there ye may be also" (John 14:1-3).

The disciples reflected a moment, then Thomas responded, "Lord, we know not whither thou goest; and how can we know the way? Jesus saith unto him, I am the way, the truth, and the life: no man cometh unto the Father, but by me" (John 14:5-6).

Any Moment Now

There are 1,845 references in the Bible to the Lord's return and no less than ninety New Testament verses signifying that Christ's coming again could occur at any time. It will happen "in a moment, in the twinkling of an eye, at the last trump: for the trumpet shall sound, and the dead shall be raised incorruptible, and we shall be changed" (1 Cor. 15:52).

Paul exhorted us to "look for the Saviour, the Lord Jesus Christ" from heaven (Phil. 3:20); for it's "unto them that look for him shall he appear" (Heb. 9:28). Jesus urged us to be looking for certain things to begin to happen. He clearly did not say that when the apocalyptical events described in Matthew 24, Mark 13 and

Luke 21 have reached their worst, believers are to look up. Rather, "when these things begin to come to pass, then look up, and lift up your heads; for your redemption draweth nigh" (Luke 21:28). The key word here is "begin." That is, when the apocalyptical signs begin to take place, such as is the case presently, we are to look for Christ's return. He further exhorted, "Watch ye therefore, and pray always, that ye may be accounted worthy to escape all these things that shall come to pass, and to stand before the Son of man" (Luke 21:36). Believers are to wait, work and watch in anticipation of Christ's return.

The Greatest Marriage

Jesus said the home-going of the church would be like a wedding. John described it as the marriage supper of the Lamb, to which believers are invited. Centuries ago the tenderhearted Scot Samuel Rutherford, who was martyred for Christ in the Aberdeen prison, wrote, "God has booked your heaven and your happiness, if you are called to the Marriage Supper of the Lamb." The *China Daily* carried a story of how 304 couples had been married in one super wedding ceremony. That's nothing compared to the numberless saints of the ages who will be present at the marriage feast of the Lamb.

When Christ comes again, the saints of all the ages will rise from the ashes and dust of cemeteries throughout the whole earth — yes, even from the depths of the oceans — to be forever with the Lord. When Christ comes for His bride, He "shall change our vile body, that it may be fashioned like unto his glorious body, according to the working whereby he is able even to subdue all things unto himself" (Phil. 3:21). Scottish martyr James Graham wrote on the window of his jail cell the night before he was burned at the stake, "Lord, since thou know'st where all these atoms are, I'm hopeful thou'lt recover my dust, and confident thou'lt raise me with the just."

With all the clues of approaching Armageddon, the actual date still remains a mystery. Yes, there are those who try to circumvent Jesus' firm word, "Ye know neither the day nor the hour wherein the Son of man cometh" (Matt. 25:13). The booklet *88 Reasons Why the Rapture Will be in 1988* was distributed to five million people. But 1988 came and went. The impossibility of accurately dating Christ's return may be for the best, as Richard Glover of China observed. Having read of end times in the Bible, he took heart: "No day is named in connection with the Second Coming of Christ, so that every day may be hallowed by the sense of the possibility of its being the day of His Advent."

On the other hand, we're cautioned that "there shall come in the last days scoffers, walking after their own lusts, and saying, Where is the promise of his coming? for since the fathers fell asleep, all things continue as they were from the beginning of the creation. For this they willingly are ignorant [that]...the day of the Lord will come as a thief in the night" (2 Pet. 3:3-5,10).

Ripe for Harvest

In the light of Christ's promise to come again at any moment, there is nothing more important for us to do than to evangelize. "Watch for...souls, as they that must give account" (Heb. 13:17). C.S. Lewis used to admonish us at Oxford to be ready for Jesus so that He would be able to say, "You were at your post when the inspection came."

Coming into the 1970s there were thirty-seven thousand Christian missionaries. Today there are sixty-two thousand. Let's keep up the increase. "Put ye in the sickle, for the harvest is ripe...multitudes, multitudes in the valley of decision: for the day of the Lord is near in the valley of decision" (Joel 3:13-14).

Former President Reagan said in the *Saturday Evening Post*, "Our responsibility begins with 'the peace the world cannot give,' the peace of spirit." This is the same peace of which Paul wrote: "Therefore being justified by faith, we have peace with God through our Lord Jesus Christ" (Rom. 5:1). Martin Luther described this peace as a rebirth experience: "When by the Spirit of God, I understood the words, 'the just shall live by faith,' I [was] born again like a new man; I entered through the open doors into the very paradise of God."

A Gallup poll cited in *Church Around the World* of December 1989 claimed, "Eighty-four percent of the population firmly believe in Jesus Christ, [while] ninety-four percent believe in God." While you may include yourself in those high figures, you must ask yourself if you believe in Jesus Christ as your personal Lord and Savior. That alone — not church attendance or Bible knowledge or general belief in God — is what determines whether or not you're a Christian, whether you will be called with the elect at Christ's return. Father Robert McDougal of Toronto recalled his previous Christian commitment as being merely a theological knowledge which "occupied me from my Adam's apple to my skull. [Now], it's Christ in me, all of me, from the soles of my feet to the crown of my head! And it's forever!"

Salvation depends solely on the fact that Jesus Christ came to earth two millennia ago to die for our sins so that we might ask Him into our hearts; when He comes again, we will go with Him, forever to be with the Lord. Whether you are a church-insider who needs to rededicate your life to Christ; a backslider who needs to return to the Lord with your whole heart; or an outsider who needs to receive Christ — I urge you to confess your sins to Christ. Do so now in the assurance that "if we confess our sins, he [Jesus Christ] is faithful and just to forgive us our sins, and to cleanse us from all unrighteousness" (1 John 1:9).

Don't conceal any of your sins, for "he that covereth his sins shall not prosper: but whoso confesseth and forsaketh them shall have mercy" (Prov. 28:13). When you confess your sins, what happens to them? "The blood of Jesus Christ his Son cleanseth us from all sin" (1 John 1:7). Hence they are gone — as far as the east is from the west — into the sea of God's forgetfulness, never again to be remembered or held against you.

Having confessed your sins, you have the guarantee that you're saved: "That if thou shalt confess with thy mouth [Jesus as Lord], and shalt believe in thine heart that God hath raised him from the dead, thou shalt be saved. For with the heart man believeth unto righteousness; and with the mouth confession is made unto salvation" (Rom. 10:9-10).

However, being a Christian carries with it the responsibility of sharing Christ with others. Jesus said, "Whosoever therefore shall confess me before men, him will I confess also before my Father which is in heaven. But whosoever shall deny me before men, him will I also deny before my Father which is in heaven" (Matt. 10:32-33).

Perhaps you'd like a confession to use, one which I've prayed with more than two hundred thousand people who have come forward to confess Jesus Christ as Savior and Lord in our crusades, as well as with millions via TV. Pray out loud, from your heart, to Jesus Christ, "God, be merciful to me, a sinner. Receive me now for Christ's sake. Cleanse me from my sin by Your precious blood, shed on the cross for me; and fill me with Your Holy Spirit. Teach me to pray each day; to read Your will for my life from Your Word, the Bible; and help me to worship and serve You in the fellowship of Your church. I thank You, Lord Jesus Christ. Amen!"

If you've made that your prayer, write to me about it. I'll send you a letter of encouragement, along with literature to help you on your way in Christ. Write to: Dr. John Wesley White, Box 501, White Pine, TN 37890; or Box 120, Markham, Ontario L3P 7R5, Canada.